Professionalism and Self-management

Social Work Skills in Practice

Series editors:
Ruben Martin, *Honorary Senior Lecturer in Social Work, University of Kent*
Alisoun Milne, *Professor of Social Gerontology and Social Work, University of Kent*

About the series:

The social work profession is constantly evolving and adjusting to changes in the policy, professional and care contexts and to wider issues such as demographic and structural shifts. Initiatives to address perceived challenges and concerns within the profession have included reforms of professional standards and regulators and reviews of social work education.

The *Social Work Skills in Practice* series aims to explore core skills and knowledge needed to practise effectively as a social worker, whether working with children and families or adult service users and their carers.

All books in the series adopt a critically reflective lens on the development and deployment of social work skills, are theoretically-grounded and evidence-informed, and address issues of relevance to all service user groups in different settings and sectors.

Titles in the series:

Professional Writing Skills: Louise Frith and Ruben Martin
Diversity, Difference and Dilemmas: Kish Bhatti-Sinclair and Chris Smethurst (eds.)
Evidence-informed Practice for Social Work: Hugh McLaughlin and Barbra Teater
Professionalism and Self-management: Godfred Boahen and Fran Wiles
Teamworking Skills for Social Workers: Ruben Martin
Critical Analysis Skills for Social Workers: David Wilkins and Godfred Boahen

Forthcoming titles:

Conflict Resolution: Brian Littlechild
Working with Networks and Communities: Martin Webber

Professionalism and Self-management

Godfred Boahen & Fran Wiles

Open University Press

Open University Press
McGraw-Hill Education
8th Floor, 338 Euston Road
London
England
NW1 3BH

www.openup.co.uk

and Two Penn Plaza, New York, NY 10121-2289, USA

First published 2019

Copyright © Open International Publishing Ltd, 2019

All rights reserved. Except for the quotation of short passages for the purposes of criticism and review, no part of this publication may be reproduced, stored in a retrieval system, or transmitted, in any form or by any means, electronic, mechanical, photocopying, recording or otherwise, without the prior written permission of the publisher or a licence from the Copyright Licensing Agency Limited. Details of such licences (for reprographic reproduction) may be obtained from the Copyright Licensing Agency Ltd of Saffron House, 6–10 Kirby Street, London EC1N 8TS.

Commissioning Editor: Vivien Antwi
Development Editor: Tom Payne
Editorial Assistant: Karen Harris
Content Product Manager: Ali Davis

A catalogue record of this book is available from the British Library

ISBN-13: 9780335263486
ISBN-10: 0335263488
eISBN: 9780335263493

Library of Congress Cataloging-in-Publication Data
CIP data applied for

Typeset by Transforma Pvt. Ltd., Chennai, India

Printed and bound by CPI Group (UK) Ltd, Croydon, CR0 4YY

Fictitious names of companies, products, people, characters and/or data that may be used herein (in case studies or in examples) are not intended to represent any real individual, company, product or event.

Praise for this book

'This text is a very useful contribution to the literature on professionalism in social work. In a series of chapters, the theoretical foundations of the range of professional skills are clearly explored, and the reader is then given the opportunity to deepen their understanding though a series of reflection points and case examples. Clearly and concisely written, it will prove of assistance to social workers in integrating theory and practice, both in the latter stages of their education and in the early years of their qualifying careers.'

Dr Martin Kettle, Senior Lecturer, Glasgow Caledonian University, UK

'This book is particularly valuable for social work students and newly-qualified social workers who want to explore professional skills and for experienced social workers wanting to refresh themselves about those skills. There is a useful exploration of various perspectives on professionalism and social work professionalism, with thought-provoking chapters on self-management, supporting people to self-manage, communication, safeguarding, risk management and leadership. A particular strength of the book is the consistent and frequent integration of practice material; for instance, there are helpful exercises, reflection points and practice examples throughout.'

Stewart Collins, Honorary Research Fellow, Bangor University and Associate Lecturer, Open University, UK

'This rich and valuable book will nourish and support those seeking to develop and deepen their social work practice. Based on an analysis of professionalism, it explains the intensely useful skills of self-management (self-awareness, critical analysis, research mindedness, emotional resilience and use of supervision amongst others) and how they can support practice in key areas such as communication, safeguarding, leadership and coproduction. Presenting a full range of models and tools, the authors enable the reader to reflect on and integrate them through carefully-considered practice examples and exercises. Written with great respect for and understanding of social work, this book will act as a resource and a companion for social workers.'

Keith Davies, Associate Professor, Kingston University London and St. George's, University of London, UK

'This timely and accessible book explores professionalism in the current context of social work practice. A real strength is the use of varied case study material to illustrate the arguments being made and to support

the application of theory, research and critical reflection in practice. It is a valuable resource for social work students, practitioners and educators in the development of relational practice skills and ethical use of professional power.'

Prof. Anna Gupta, Professor of Social Work, Royal Holloway, University of London, UK

'The status and regard afforded to social work as a profession and to individual members of the profession varies between places and moments in history. However, it is fair to say that in the UK, and in England in particular, social work has experienced much state intervention and change that may adversely affect the standing of the profession, whatever the stated intentions by decision makers. In addition, the very unique professional role that social workers have, with its intrinsically relationship-based approach and reflective, intelligent use of self, working with people at their most vulnerable moments, means that social workers will benefit from reminders and further learning that this clear and accessible text provides. This book will appeal to many with its "applied" but intellectually-robust approach and the frequent "pause and reflect" points throughout. Placing an emphasis upon self-management and skills, including higher-order skills such as reflection and critical analysis, makes a very helpful contribution to an important area of focus: professional identification, professional standing and appropriate professional "pride" in the work of social workers for the benefit of those with whom we work and for the profession as a whole.'

Cath Holmström, Deputy Head of School, School of Applied Social Science, University of Brighton, UK

Contents

Foreword

When Ruben Martin and I conceived of this series, our overriding ambition was to ensure that all of the books contained within it would have a clear and coherent focus on social work *skills*. Through our teaching, research and careers in practice, we identified a need to better equip students and social workers with the competencies required to make a positive impact on the lives of service users and their families.

The series is considerably strengthened by the addition of *Professionalism and Self-management* by Godfred Boahen and Fran Wiles. The book makes a unique contribution, offering a mix of theory and evidence about social work professionalism alongside practice-based material for the development of social work skills. The authors offer a detailed analysis of what professional social work skills 'look like', their form and function, and what distinctively defines the professional social work skill set and value base. Their narrative offers a helpful and positive counter to the dominant managerialist agenda and reminds us of the expertise of social workers and the contribution they make to the lives and well-being of service users and their families. They helpfully organize the book so that the initial chapters set the 'conceptual scene' and provide a foundation for the whole text. The more practice-oriented focus of the remaining chapters then offers the reader thought-provoking insights into the skills and values that make up contemporary social work, how to balance what are often competing tensions and demands, and the importance of engaging with a rich mix of skills, methods and approaches to effectively meet the often complex and varied needs of service users.

Throughout the book, Boahen and Wiles adopt an accessible yet authoritative tone engaging with practice issues and case examples alongside theoretical and sociological contributions. They remind us of social work's place in the world, its identity, ambition and challenges. At a time when professionalism is being attacked politically and publicly – when it is increasingly required to 'prove itself' – this book offers a robust and well-evidenced case for, to use their own words, 'further developing a sense of being a cohesive and durable profession'. The book provides a valuable and rich source of knowledge about professionalism and self-management in social work and has much to offer both social work education and practice.

Alisoun Milne, Professor of Social Gerontology and Social Work, School of Social Policy, Sociology and Social Research (SSPSSR), University of Kent, UK

About the series editors

Ruben Martin is an Honorary Senior Lecturer in Social Work at the University of Kent's SSPSSR. Since retiring from his full-time post, he has continued part-time work as a lecturer, tutor, consultant, independent practice educator, writer and editor. He has authored *Teamworking Skills* and, with Louise Frith, co-authored *Professional Writing Skills* in this *Social Work Skills in Practice* series. After completing a professional social work qualification at the University of Leicester, Ruben initially worked as a probation officer, and then as a social work lecturer from 1979 to 1983 on a CQSW programme at Leicester Polytechnic. Moving to the voluntary sector, he was national training manager for The Salvation Army Social Services. He returned to lecturing on a DipSW programme in 1995 and became a lecturer at the University of Kent in 2003, where he was Director of Studies for the B.A. programme for six years. He is registered with the Health and Care Professions Council (HCPC). Ruben's academic interests include social work skills and practice learning.

Dr Alisoun Milne is Professor of Social Gerontology and Social Work at the University of Kent's SSPSSR. Alisoun is widely published in both academic- and practice-related journals and attracts research funding from sources such as the NIHR School for Social Care Research. Her key research interests are: social work with older people and their families; older carers and dementia carers; mental health in later life; and long-term care. Alisoun also has managerial responsibilities for social work developments, including a regional Social Work Teaching Partnership, and contributes to delivering both undergraduate and postgraduate qualifying programmes. Alisoun was a member of the Standing Commission on Carers for the duration of its existence and was on the Executive Committee of the British Society of Gerontology from 2009—15. She is currently a member of the Association of Professors of Social Work (APSW),the Chief Social Worker for Adults Advisory Group, and the Research Excellence Framework 2021 sub-panel for Social Work and Social Policy. Before becoming an academic in 1995, Alisoun worked as a social worker and team manager in two London boroughs; she is registered with the HCPC.

1 Introduction

In this book, part of the *Social Work Skills in Practice* series, we aim to explore professionalism within the context of social work and, in particular, what professional social work skills 'look like'. We have written this book to offer a counter-argument to what we see as an ongoing trend in recent years to 'de-professionalize' social work. This trend, which arguably began in the 1980s, has emphasized the need for greater government control of social work (and of social workers), thus leaving less space for autonomous professional activity.

'De-professionalization' can be seen as part of a broader re-design of the public sector across the UK and much of the Western world based on 'managerialism', which is a process through which practice outcomes are determined by performance indicators, bureaucratic procedures and the adaptation of business practices from the private sector in the delivery of public services. This, in turn, is linked to New Public Management (NPM) – the belief that welfare services should function like businesses, which seek to reduce losses and make profits or, at the very least, breakeven (opponents of NPM argue, however, that welfare services should be seen as 'public goods', which should be provided irrespective of whether they are unprofitable). The problem with a managerialist approach to social work is that it undermines the professional skills and expertise of individual social workers. It also risks the fragmentation of social work into a series of distinctive tasks or roles – such as child protection, adult mental health or working with disabled children – rather than recognizing the profession as a shared set of values and skills.

Fortunately, there is nothing inevitable about this fragmentation of social work or, indeed, of any profession. For example, when considering the medical profession, although doctors may practice in a great variety of settings – in GP surgeries, in Accident & Emergency (A&E) departments, in care homes, in the delivery of vaccines to remote areas, in rural areas of the developing world – they are all perceived as being medical professionals. Having said this, it may not be immediately clear as to *why* this should be the case. After all, a doctor in an A&E department is not likely to spend much of his or her time administering vaccines, unlike a doctor operating in rural communities in less socio-economically-advantaged parts of the world, who may spend more time managing the logistical demands of travelling into remote areas and ensuring that vaccines are transported safely and in good condition. Nevertheless, in both these examples, it is evident that, in a broad sense, *medical practice* is taking place. There is something, then, about the shared endeavour of medical professionals that somehow binds them together and becomes more important than, for instance, the day-to-day activities of individual doctors. And if this is possible for medical (and other) professions, then we would assert that it is equally possible for us, as social workers, to demonstrate that we too have a shared endeavour, something that, despite initial appearances, we are all engaged in together. This is what we consider as *professionalism*.

Besides conceptualizing professionalism as a set of unifying values for social work, we suggest that self-management is another important domain of 'being a professional'. As we will show in Chapter 3, self-management refers to people's ability to oversee their own care after initial training; in social work, this implies the ability to manage the emotional demands of the job, plan and seek training, and understand the appropriate conduct expected of professional social workers. In this respect, professionalism and self-management interact in many ways, for instance, reflection skills, being proactive yet accountable, and the capacity for empowering service users to self-manage their care. Our argument here is not to downplay the duties of organizations to train and develop social workers; rather, we aim to show that self-management skills are prerequisites for being professional.

Approach and style of the book

Our key aim, and that of the *Social Work Skills in Practice* series, is to translate, as far as is practicable, the theory and evidence about social work professionalism into a helpful learning tool for the development of skills for practice. Although we engage in theoretical or research-based discussions, we adopt an informative and accessible tone with the aim of contextualizing key debates within social work skills. For example, if one is acting in a professional manner as a social worker in a family court setting, what does that mean? What might that 'look like' and what skills might be required? And, does professionalism mean the same in any context, look the same or require the same set of skills as conducting research as a social worker, setting up a community housing project, or providing counselling and support in the aftermath of a natural disaster (to name just a few examples of the different tasks and activities that social workers might engage in)?

Thus, unsurprisingly, we focus predominately on 'real-life' practice scenarios and dilemmas. We have included many examples of practical and self-assessment tasks that we would encourage you, the reader, to complete, either individually or in groups (such as in group supervision sessions or perhaps as part of a team awayday). While we recommend that readers start with Chapters 1 and 2, because the conceptual discussions there on professionalism and self-management provide the foundations for the rest of the book, it may be that for you, personally, the latter chapters are more immediately useful. This is because after Chapter 2, the writing is deliberately *practice-focused* — we apply important ideas and theories of social work professionalism to practice. This may mean that these chapters resonate more with your experience, incentivizing you to prioritize them over the theoretical discussions.

Having said this, we believe it would be a mistake to try and emphasize the unity and shared endeavour of the social work profession, while at the same time writing chapters that focus narrowly on this or that area (such as child protection or statutory services in the UK more generally). Consequently, while we have noted that the more skills-focused chapters may more readily chime with everyday practice experience, we also suggest that some skills may assume more importance at different career points. For instance, leadership, when acting in management, or safeguarding, when in a designated child or adult protection role. It may be that with time, within any given social work career, one or more of these skill sets might be foregrounded while others take more of a 'supporting' role.

Overview of the chapters

We have divided the chapters into those that explore the theoretical foundations and history of social work as well as the current debates in the literature, from those that will more directly assist you in honing your professional skills in social work. While the former chapters may be more useful for those readers approaching this text from an academic setting (with the latter chapters more appropriate to professional social workers and those interested in pursuing a career in the field), these are contextualized within, and applied to, the everyday skills that all social workers need to develop in order to be effective in their many and varied roles. The goal of these praxis-oriented chapters is to enable social workers to develop the skills commensurate with the term 'professional'.

Of course, we are not the first to suggest that social work is a profession (rather than a set of activities or a craft). In the UK and Western nations, developments since the late 1990s may even raise questions about why we are worried about the de-professionalization of social work. After all, there have been significant policy changes: the legal protection of the term 'social worker', a shift in the educational requirements for social workers from diploma-level to degree-level, recognition of the need for national regulation of social workers, and an increase in membership of the British Association of Social Workers (BASW), the professional body in the UK. However, while there are many positive aspects to these developments, they could also be interpreted as (further) attempts to increase government control of social work. In other words, professionalism may not be incontrovertibly a 'good thing' if it increases social workers' power and concomitantly leads to more political control.

Type of content	Chapter number	Description of the chapter
Theoretical chapters	**2**	Chapter 2 is the first of the theoretical chapters, where we explore some of the key questions about the nature and implications of professionalism, drawing on the sociological and philosophical literature. We also consider what professionalism might mean within the context of multidisciplinary settings, especially as these kinds of arrangements are both in development (for example, in the form of child protection Multi-Agency Safeguarding Hubs) and disappearing (for example, in adult mental health services).
	3	Here, we take the context of the discussion in **Chapter 2** and focus on self-management as another dimension of professionalism. Alongside recognition as a profession, it is expected that social workers will exhibit greater autonomy over their work including planning their training and development needs, showing accountability for their career progression, and skilfully managing the emotional demands of their roles. We highlight self-efficacy and emotional intelligence in this regard.

Taken together, **Chapters 2** and **3** focus on theoretical and contextual explorations of professionalism that lay the foundations for the rest of the book. From **Chapter 4** onwards, we cover the practical, skills-based application or interpretation of the concept of professionalism in social work.

Type of content	Chapter number	Description of the chapter
Skills-based chapters	**4**	In **Chapter 4**, we identify and debate what we regard as the key skills and values congruent with social work professionalism – skills of self-management, communication, dealing with risk, safeguarding and leadership. Within this discussion, we will consider how social workers are often faced with dilemmas and competing demands, and how the skills and values of the social work profession may come into conflict with one another as they are exposed to the realities of practice.

Type of content	Chapter number	Description of the chapter
Skills-based chapters	**5**	In **Chapter 5**, we explore the skills and values related to supporting and enabling self-management in people who use social work services. The point here is that, in modern social work, practitioners deal with people who require intervention because of problematic behaviours. In this work, changing their lifestyles is a prerequisite for successful outcomes. On the other hand, as epitomized by the rise of user movements, some people simply want social workers to provide them with information and advice or work alongside them as equal partners in resolving their difficulties. Thus, in Chapter 5 we consider motivational interviewing, goal-setting and partnership working as skills for enabling people to self-manage their care.
	6	In **Chapter 6** – as in Chapter 5 – we explore the skills and values necessary for 'good' communication in social work, and in particular what might be called the 'art of communicating' as a professional, whether this be in written form, when speaking (to whom?), when exchanging views with others or when imparting one's 'professional opinion'.
	7	In **Chapter 7**, we move onto considering the skills and values related to safeguarding and how dealing with or managing risk can place unique demands on social work practitioners. As noted, this chapter does not focus on child protection or adult protection in particular; instead, it takes a wider view of risk than 'only' abuse or neglect. Thus, in this chapter we consider how managing risk is – as with the other skills discussed in Chapters 4–8 – a core activity in the social work profession, and how this may place considerable emotional demand on individual social workers.
	8	We discuss leadership skills and values as they relate to social work professionalism in **Chapter 8**, not simply the values of leadership-as-management but of social work as a leadership profession. We examine what this might mean in practice and how the differing skills of social workers might (or might not) lend themselves to the development of professional leadership.

Type of content	Chapter number	Description of the chapter
	9	In seeking to build on the various case studies and practical examples of the preceding chapters, we introduce two extended case studies in **Chapter 9**. These are intended to provide a reflective and analytical space for readers, either individually or in groups, to apply the skills of professionalism we discuss throughout the book.
	10	In **Chapter 10**, we conclude the book by drawing together some of the common themes and strands from the previous nine chapters, while also highlighting what we see as the main challenges for social work, as a collective and as a collection of individuals, in maintaining and further developing a sense of being a cohesive and durable profession.

2 What is professionalism?

Chapter overview

By the end of this chapter, you will:

- Understand the historical origins of social work as a profession
- Identify professionalism as a multi-faceted concept with different meanings in various contexts
- Understand professionalism as a form of socialization, culture and discourse
- Relate the issues discussed to your own practice

Introduction

In this chapter, we explore the concept of professionalism by drawing on the sociological and philosophical literature, where in the former there is a long-standing history of researching the topic. Taking this disciplinary approach, we conceptualize **professionalization** as *the process through which an occupation gains and exerts more control and power over its work* (Freidson 2001). As we will show, this process can emanate from within the profession or from outside. Our conceptual exposition will then form the background for us to engage with the current policy debates about the need to *professionalize* social work using England as a case study – we will show how these recent developments would impact social workers, service users and employers.

Social work as a profession – a brief history

The term 'professionalism' derives from the concepts of 'profession' or 'professional', which in everyday usage convey the image of competence, trustworthiness, high-quality service and autonomous decision-making. These lay understandings can be traced to sociologists from Western Europe and the USA in the post-War period, who accorded state agents altruistic motives (Freidson 1994). It was arguably during this period that citizens in most Western European nations had the greatest belief in the welfare state and the power of the state to do 'good'. At this time, it was felt that some occupations – for instance, civil servants, teachers, doctors and lawyers – benefited the wider public because they helped maintain public order and the efficient running of the state. It is therefore not surprising that at this point when professionals had a positive image, various occupations, including social work, actively sought the title 'professional'.

One helpful way of understanding the process whereby a collection of people doing the same job become a 'profession' is that the noun refers to the group's acquired status whereas 'professionalization' describes the practices through which occupational groups sought, attained and maintained the status of 'profession' (Evetts 2003). It is also worth holding onto the sociological thought that these developments occurred either from within the occupational groups or were imposed by more powerful actors, such as governments. For instance, the leaders of a trade body could decide that they wanted to 'improve' the image of their members, and so they would enact policies to this end. Alternatively, as has occurred to social work practice several times, the government could aim to elevate the skills base of the workforce, and specify minimum qualification and training standards.

Specifically with social work, the quest for recognition was given impetus by the Local Authority Social Services Act 1970 (Buchanan 2011), which established local authority social services committees and elevated the status of social workers, as noted by one commentator on the Act:

> In the past few months the remuneration offered to senior social workers has been doubled and even trebled by local authorities which have anticipated the present Act; and for the first time in the history of the profession a qualified social worker can look forward eventually to securing a salary and status comparable with those of a bank manager, professor, assistant secretary or county court judge.
>
> (Harris 1970: 532)

However, it should also be highlighted that this Act marked the beginning of statutory regulation of social work and henceforth, with each newly-publicized deficiency in practice, governments would enact policies to increase the skills base of the profession of social work. At the time, this landmark legislation was received well by some in the charity sector, who had been calling for more efficient delivery of services with a greater emphasis on a 'scientific' approach to measuring their impact.

Ironically, as social work was gaining professional status, the term 'profession' came under sustained attack from Anglo-American sociologists. In his seminal work, *Professionalism Reborn: Theory, Prophecy and Policy*, Freidson (1994) termed the 1960s onwards as the 'critical period' for the study of the professions. This is because researchers challenged the notion of professionals as employees interested in 'doing good'. According to Freidson, it was argued that professionals were self-interested in protecting their employment privileges and their closeness to the state granted them legal powers to exercise authority over others. This criticism work implied that by seeking and acquiring the status of a profession, groups could make unsubstantiated claims about their vocational worth and sustain their influence by controlling a particular area of work and, through this, they prevented competition from other occupations.

On a more positive note, Freidson considered that becoming a profession was another way for the group to ensure quality of service. This could be achieved through setting out entry requirements such as standards of training – so, for instance, the term 'social worker' could only be used by people who had completed the requisite training. Alternatively, a group could set out minimum service standards and outline what clients could expect of them; those who sought membership therefore implicitly consented to abide by these standards and expectations and demonstrate that they had the skills to fulfil them.

In the 1980s, during the ascendancy of free-market ideas, professions were criticized for stifling employment competition and seeking to protect their interests in opposition to that of service users (Freidson 2001). With respect to social work, a notable policy development in that decade was the Barclay Report (1982). While ostensibly aimed at setting out ideas to improve social work practice, it propagated the market-orientated dogma of the time about the need to 'ration' scarce resources. Taking the position that resources were limited and had to be rationed by social workers (Hallett 1983), the Barclay Report aimed to prescribe the duties of social workers within this constraint.

It can be argued therefore that the Barclay Report's analyses still resonate today – some of the tasks performed by social workers are increasingly discharged by 'unqualified' staff, for instance. Simultaneously, there have been attempts to elevate the standing of social work because, as we stated earlier, certain professions are essential to how the state discharges its duties. Social work is an important part of the welfare state because the profession is imbued with certain duties – for instance, by law in England only social workers can lead safeguarding work with both children and adults. Additionally, social workers are important channels for the state to allocate resources and separate out those who are considered to deserve help from those who are not.

Therefore, ironically, while the knowledge and skills of the profession are frequently attacked by the media and politicians as lacking, concurrently there are attempts made to elevate the standing of the occupational group.

New Labour: (re)professionalizing social work?

Arguably, it was the UK Labour administration from 1997 that introduced statutory mechanisms to (re)professionalize social work through concerted attempts to increase the skills of the workforce. One way by which this was achieved was increased regulation, which focused on who could be a social worker, the level of 'competencies' that they ought to display and what they could do in practice. An undergraduate degree became the minimum requirement for social work accreditation, whereas in the past entry was by means of a diploma. The Labour government also accorded legal protection to the term 'social worker' – thus, just like 'solicitor' or 'doctor', only those who had the appropriate qualification could practice under that title. New Labour also created and maintained a register of social workers, and the General Social Care Council (GSCC) was established in 2001 to set out and review minimum standards of competencies. It was also in 2001 that the Social Care Institute for Excellence (SCIE) was set up to harness a knowledge base as the bedrock of workforce competence. All these were given impetus by various inquiries held after tragic deaths of children known to children's services that highlighted deficiencies in current practice (for example, Victoria Climbié).

These policy initiatives were motivated by the assumption that, for a discipline to acquire the status of profession, it had to lay claim to a distinct set of knowledge. In the case of social work, compared with allied professions such as doctors, nurses or psychologists, there was not an identifiable body of theoretical approaches or evidence-base of knowledge that practitioners could draw upon in interventions. Another argument was that it was difficult to distinguish the set of skills that social workers deployed in their work from those of allied professions. This presupposition led to pressure for social work academics and practitioners to justify their unique professional status. Another development flowing from the previous point about the lack of an identifiable body of knowledge is that, arguably since the late 1990s, there has been a concerted effort to delineate the distinct nature of social work knowledge, theory and practice in relation to the other 'caring' professions. (See, for instance, Payne [2005, 2006] and Shaw [2009] for debates about the distinctiveness of social work theory and research.)

The 2011 Coalition and social work: continuities and change in professionalization

The Coalition government, which operated between 2010 and 2015, initiated reviews of social work. Maintaining the historical trend, another tragic death of a child, this time of Peter Connolly ('Baby P'), led to the formation of the Social Work Taskforce (SWT) to review the conduct of social work and suggest 'reforms'. This inquiry subsequently led to the formation of the Social Work Reform Board (SWRB) to improve practice. In a revolutionary proposal, the SWRB created the Professional Capabilities Framework (PCF), which:

> . . . clearly set[s] out how a social worker's knowledge, skills and capacity build over time as they move through their careers. As a first step in developing this framework, the Reform Board proposes that there are nine core social work capabilities which should be relevant, to a greater or lesser degree, to all social workers and social work students no matter their level of experience or the setting they work in.
>
> (SWRB 2010: 6)

In the context of present discussion, we will argue that the PCF is unique because it sets out in policy what should be considered as the yardsticks of professionalism in social work. Hitherto in the literature, writers have sought to outline normative standards, or what professionalism would look like if it were 'real'. The PCF moves this debate on by stipulating what a professional social worker *has to be* or the expectations that they should meet.

As has been well discussed in the literature, the PCF outlines nine 'domains' of 'capabilities'. Students or practising social workers should demonstrate that they could achieve these within the trajectory of their employment. Thus, 'capabilities' is deliberately chosen instead of 'competencies', as the former is deemed to convey a more forward-looking assessment of an individual professional's skill set (Taylor and Bogo 2014). We discuss this further in Chapter 4; however, in the interim, we want to explore further the PCF's definition of professionalism. The professionalism domain for qualified social workers stipulates that:

> Social workers are members of an internationally recognised profession, a title protected in UK law. Social workers demonstrate professional commitment by taking responsibility for their conduct, practice and learning, with support through supervision. As representatives of the social work profession they safeguard its reputation and are accountable to the professional regulator.
>
> - Be able to meet the requirements of the professional regulator
> - Promote the profession in a growing range of contexts
> - Take responsibility for obtaining regular, effective supervision from a manager for effective practice, reflection and career development
> - Maintain professionalism in the face of more challenging circumstances
> - Manage workload independently, seeking support and suggesting solutions for workload difficulties
> - Maintain appropriate personal/professional boundaries in more challenging circumstances
> - Make skilled use of self as part of your interventions
> - Maintain awareness of own professional limitations and knowledge gaps. Establish a network of internal and external colleagues from whom to seek advice and expertise
> - Identify and act on learning needs for CPD, including through supervision
> - Routinely promote well-being at work
> - Raise and address issues of poor practice, internally through the organisation, and then independently if required.
>
> (BASW [2012] 'Professional Capabilities Framework – Social Work Level Capabilities'. Available at: https://www.basw.co.uk/pcf/PCF05SocialWorkLevelCapabilities.pdf [accessed 14th May 2018])

We would like to point out to readers that the England-specific policies, including the PCF, that we argue have led to the push to 'professionalize' social work have resonance for our international counterparts and allied occupations such as teaching. In the Introduction, we briefly mentioned the debates about the status of social work. These can be seen within the context of New Public Management (NPM), which has gained ascendancy in most liberal democracies. Under NPM, there is an emphasis on the efficient delivery of statutory services, and a strong belief that they could achieve better outcomes if they were ran as businesses. The service user is considered a 'consumer' who has 'choice' and, if they were allowed to exercise preference, then 'producers' would be more attuned to their needs and in the process become cheaper and more 'responsive' to demand. Taking this to its logical conclusion, it means that social workers (and public sector employees more broadly) are required to become more professional in the corporate sense and 'skilled' at the process of providing services. However, the value-base of the profession sometimes contradicted the ethos of market forces – for instance, whereas NPM does not necessarily perceive socio-economic inequality as 'bad', social workers opposed it on ethical grounds. Thus, in the 1980s, when free-market ideas gained ascendancy, professional groups were attacked by governments, particularly in the Anglo-Saxon countries (including the UK and USA), for using their power to prevent further marketization of services. Bringing the discussion back to the UK context, the then Conservative-led Government considered social work to be more left wing and therefore obstructive to its policy aims of reducing the size of the welfare state and increasing competition in the provision of services.

Summary

- There have been long-standing attempts to 'professionalize' social work both by governments and from within the profession.
- In England The Local Authority Social Services Act 1970 can be considered the most significant point in this quest because it established social work as a statutory role, created social services committees and outlined their duties.
- The New Labour government enhanced legal protection for the title 'social work' – thus it would be illegal for anyone to afford him or herself this title if they did not have the associated university degree.
- The Coalition government, through the Professional Capabilities Framework, entrenched in policy the view that social work is a profession, but the debate now is between specialization and generic qualification.

Up to this point, our historical discussion, although brief, shows that the occupational status of social work has been subject to various contentions since the post-War period. Not long after the Second World War, like most public-sector employment, social work sought to be recognized as a profession to benefit from the positive image accorded vocations so classified. However, once it gained statutory recognition in the 1970s, social work became an intensely political profession, and with each publicized practice deficiency, there were calls to increase the skill base of the workforce. These issues are long-standing, and many complex and challenging questions for the profession of social work, including 'what is professionalism?' We will answer this question by analysing the theoretical literature in the next section.

Exploring the current meaning of 'professionalism'

Moving on from the historical exposition, in this section we examine some current conceptualizations of professionalism. We are influenced here by the sociological literature because our position is that **professionalism** is *an identity that is ascribed to a group by external powers or through the work of the membership.*

Moreover, professionalism is not a tangible or sensible thing, something that can be seen or touched in the world, but rather a classification that emanates from social relations, either at the governmental level through legislation or professional standards, or through how various groups in society associate with each other intersubjectively.

Having said this, we must also point out that some researchers argue that the concept of 'profession' has little analytic value because so many occupations claim the title that it is difficult, or perhaps unnecessary, to ascertain its unique character (Evetts 2014). If you are sympathetic to this, then the work of the SWRB is not necessarily radical – one would take the position that the PCF is in keeping with the growing trend for every vocation to self-identify as a profession. On the other hand, there are those who argue that there is an alternative, 'real' reason why groups seek to define themselves and be recognized as such. According to this argument, even if the term 'profession' is claimed by most jobs and therefore means little, there is a pertinent point in understanding why they do so. One theory is that professionalism is a means of controlling the workforce through discourse (Evetts 2012).

Professionalism as a discourse

The term 'discourse', as it is used in social theory, derives its meaning from the work of the French philosopher Foucault, who conceptualized it as 'practices that systematically form the objects of which they speak' (1972: 49). In the Foucauldian sense, discourse has a different meaning or exposition to the everyday understanding of the concept: it is another way that power is manifested in people's lives. As Mills has explained, '[discourse] is something which produces something else (an utterance, concept, an effect), rather than something which exists in and of itself and which can be analysed in isolation' (2004: 17). Foucault considered discourse to include a set of practices and institutions that circumscribe perceptions of reality and, in this sense, discourse can even determine how individuals think of themselves. In this way, discourse impacts on how we conceive of reality because it shapes our understanding of the world.

If we take social work practice as an example, there are certain words and languages that we use that are only understandable within the context of practice: most people outside social work may not understand that when social workers say 'assessment', they mean a process related to a 'referral', usually followed by 'commissioning' services or going before a 'panel'. In the social work world, however, these words mean something, they have practical corollaries – if a manager or even computer system indicates that the 'deadline' for the 'assessment' is approaching, this usually causes a response in the professional such as 'booking a home visit' or 'arranging a joint visit' with another person.

At the risk of oversimplification, a discourse may therefore be seen as the practices, language or organizational arrangements that cause us to understand the world in a certain way. Thus, when professionalism is described as a form of discourse, the argument is that people evoke or invoke it to achieve other purposes, such as gaining the attention of managers and governments or even to attract applicants to the occupational group (Evetts 2012). Applied to our current context of the meaning of professionalism in social work, professionalism as discourse means that there is a set of institutional arrangements that sustain (and shape) the belief of social work as a profession. First, for example, you have to attend an organization called a 'university', do placements and pass, register your name with the professional regulatory body, and then frequently prove that you are worthy of the job title by accruing CPD records. Recalling the earlier point that Foucault considered discourse to be a form of *power*, when applied to social work, professionalism could be seen as a way of exercising some authority. It could be argued that the historical development of policy, such as the Local Authority Social Services Act 1970, is a manifestation of power: various governments have proposed who should be a social worker, what they should do in their profession and, equally importantly, how the job (and/or tasks) of social work should be organized by employers.

The preceding discussion shows that professionalism implies a set of practices that individuals must follow once they are designated 'professional'. These practices are reinforced by the power of certain institutions to determine the requisite practices and maintain their adherence. In the case of social work, these institutions include: the regulators who produce guidance that shapes professional conduct and practice standards; government departments, which allocate budgets and pass legislation that determine professionals' duties; and employers, who draw up employment procedures.

At the individual level, one influential Foucault scholar has coined the phrase 'governing at a distance' to explain how power shapes the behaviour of people in invisible ways (Rose and Miller 1992). We accept that there is the expectation for us to act in a certain manner, even away from our workplaces. We behave as if we are still in the office being watched by colleagues or in homes being observed by service users, our conduct being assessed to determine whether we are being 'professional'. In Foucault's thought, therefore, the various Codes of Practice in social work could be considered as discourse because practitioners are governed by them through the social relations to which they are conducive. Furthermore, these Codes regulate our understandings of what is 'proper' conduct, even if we may not agree with them or when no one is watching us to ascertain that we are (or are not) acting according to the Code.

Research note: Interpreting professionalism

A recent Health and Care Professions Council-sponsored research project (Morrow et al. 2014) involved three groups of healthcare professionals (chiropodists/podiatrists, occupational therapists and paramedics) and their educators to explore their understanding of professionalism. While not including social workers, this study is relevant to our present discussion because it addresses the subject matter of recent policy aims to professionalize social work. Also, as there is no corresponding research involving social workers, it is important to explore the view of related professions to social work.

Methodologically, twenty focus groups were conducted. The interviewers taped the conversations, transcribed them and coded the data to identify relevant themes. Unsurprisingly (given our ongoing explorations), the researchers found that the study participants did not agree on the definition of professionalism. Some of the explanations provided included technical expertise and competence but, interestingly, the participants also defined professionalism more expansively to include how the person presented themselves such as through their clothing at work. Some of the respondents who were educators even believed that professionalism encompassed how professionals conducted themselves *outside* of office hours – professionalism as 'a way of life' (2014: 15).

Reflection point 2.1

Reading Foucault, we could say that these research participants are demonstrating 'power at a distance' (Rose and Miller 1992). This is because they have taken on the discourse 'professional' and it is now shaping their conduct in all aspects of their lives. They believe that to be a professional they ought to dress in a particular way or conduct themselves in a certain manner, even when they are not at work ('a way of life').

Although it could be argued that, as social work is a profession underpinned by ethical claims to do 'good' or 'right', this should be reflected in the conduct of social workers at all times, it is a point worthy of reflection that how we conceptualize professionalism may be furtively influencing how we practise and understand social work and the skills relevant to this form of care. We should ask ourselves how this may impact on the mental health of social workers, how sustainable it is to pursue a (strenuous) standard of professionalism in all things – whether at the bar or in a traditional work setting – and what can be done to ensure a more healthful work–life balance.

We conclude this section with questions for further reflection. When reflecting on the different ways in which research participants defined professionalism, notice how these resonate with you in your current or future social work roles. To what extent does professionalism refer to your expertise and competence? Does being professional include paying attention to how you present yourself in terms of dress, behaviour and attitude? Should professionalism be confined to your working hours, or is it something that goes with you into everyday life?

Professionalism as culture

Evans, writing from the perspective of educational research, conceptualized professionalism as a form of culture where 'implicit in the interpretation – with its focus on ideology and a special set of institutions – is homogeneity of values and viewpoints' (2008: 6). Evans' postulation draws our attention to the fact that social workers generally tend to have a shared understanding of the world and common attitudes as to how issues should be resolved. Most social workers tend to believe that socio-economic inequality, rather than the inherent characteristics of service users, causes people to need assistance from statutory services. We also share similar ethics, such as that it is right that society safeguards the welfare of the poor. The question following from Evans' theorization therefore is how individuals who do not know each other, when they qualify as social workers, come to attain commonalities in their perceptions of the world and how it should be organized.

Theorists of culture highlight individual–group interaction: the collective is taken as symbolizing the 'culture', which is influenced by the actions of the discrete personalities of the community. In social work, at the level of the group, through training, reading about the essence of social work and mixing with colleagues, we undergo a process of socialization into the profession (Miller, 2010). In a similar way, we could theorize the PCF as creating a professional culture because it stipulates the values, personal qualities and skills that we should exhibit as social workers. While education may be considered the 'formal' form of being socialized into social work culture, there are also informal channels, such as the private conversations we have with managers about the way to do things and the oral history of the profession that colleagues and service users inculcate in us. However, at the personal level, we come into the profession with our own understandings of the world. Clark (2006), for instance, argues that some people are attracted into social work in the first place because of their moral character and their belief in the potential role of social work to shape society for the better.

Thus professionalism, if considered as a culture, encompasses three processes:

- First, it refers to the collective identity of the profession.
- Second, it refers to how the individual social worker manifests this collective identity in their everyday practice.
- And third, it includes the feedback loop by which this collective identity is transmitted back into the social work community's understanding of itself. This latter process would involve membership organizations such as the BASW or the International Federation of Social Workers (IFSW). Within these forums, professionals exchange knowledge about practice, debate and contribute to evolving policy, and form (new) aspirations for the profession.

Exercise 2.1: Exploring the meaning of professionalism

In the preceding section, we examined current theorisations of professionalism and applied them to recent policy developments in English social work. To deepen your understanding, consider these questions:

- What is the meaning of professionalism adopted within the PCF?
- Which sociological understandings of professionalism have we discussed?
- What are the advantages of professionalism for social work?

As readers will notice from our citation of the definition of professionalism contextualized within the PCF, the concept also means taking individual responsibility for ensuring that your practice skills and conduct meet high standards. This does not mean that professionalism is a purely individual matter: social workers are expected to actively seek out appropriate support and supervision. Professionalism therefore also involves engaging with others to collectively uphold and promote the values and reputation of the profession as a whole. Sociological theories highlight that professionalism is an ascribed identity, conferred in part by external power (though also by our own collective understandings and institutions) such as legislation and through belonging to a professional body. Sociologically, therefore, the concept of professionalism can be viewed as a means of controlling social workers through standards, codes and implicit expectations, which shape our practice and behaviour. Alternatively, professionalism can be seen as a culture – shared values, attitudes and behaviours – into which we are socialized. Professional culture implies a positive collective identity that is continually shaped by its members. These theoretical meanings are not mutually exclusive: elements of both 'control' and 'culture' explanations may have struck a chord with you as a current or aspiring social worker. Our argument in this book is that professionalism has clear advantages for social work: guiding our everyday practice and offering us a potentially supportive collective identity. These ideas are explored in the rest of this chapter.

Professionalism from 'within' and 'without'

Evetts (2003, 2006, 2012) offers an alternative understanding of professionalism – that of an identity that occurs from 'within' or 'without'. In the former, it is the workers who organize themselves to advocate for their profession to attain recognition. In the latter, in contrast, control is imposed by managers as a way of elevating the standing of their occupation and, arguably, the competence of that group of employees. Expanding further on the theme, Evetts proposes two further ways by which an occupation attains professionalism. We find it helpful to cite her work here at length because of its clear exposition:

> *Organisational professionalism* is a discourse of control used increasingly by managers in work organisations. It incorporates rational–legal forms of authority and hierarchical structures of responsibility and decision-making. It involves the increased standardization of work procedures and practices and managerialist controls. It relies on externalized forms of regulation and accountability measures such as target-setting and performance review. In contrast, and again as an ideal-type, *occupational professionalism* is a discourse constructed within professional occupational groups and incorporates collegial authority. It involves relations of practitioner trust from both employ-

> ers and clients. It is based on autonomy and discretionary judgement and assessment by practitioners in complex cases.
>
> (Evetts 2012: 6)

We would argue that Evetts' theorization is a more useful way of understanding professionalism than conceiving of it as a culture because it draws our attention to the possibility that acquiring the status is not zero-sum. Instead, whether professionalism is advantageous really depends on how and why the occupation has gained that identity. For instance, if professionalism occurs from within or if occupational professionalism is achieved, then professionals stand to benefit from having more autonomy over their work. The assumption is that members of the occupational group identify (high) standards of work, believe that each member meets them and, furthermore, that they can self-regulate their high standards. Moreover, the employers and 'clients', which in social work are the government, charities, local authorities and service users, believe in the workforce's ability to meet this desired level of quality. Implicit in this latter point is that the professional group has some power to regulate its members and, concomitantly, it can resist outside interference. In contrast, if the title of professionalism is imposed externally, the profession becomes subject to outside control, with increasing regulation over how it discharges its duties.

Applying these conceptual ideas to social work, the field has witnessed professionalism from 'without', accompanied by increased organizational control. While there have been previous attempts, in policy terms, it is arguably only through the recent work by the SWRB that 'professionalism' is stipulated as the core identity for qualified and trainee social workers. This development marks an attempt not only to shape the behaviour of social workers, but also provide normative standards by which social workers and others can evaluate their conduct. Furthermore, it is argued that in order to satisfy the new demands of professionalism, educational (and training) standards of social workers ought to be as high as those of more established professions such as medicine. Implicit in this is the supposition that there is a hierarchy of professionals, of which social work is not pre-eminent. Consequently, the aim is to equip all social workers with the requisite skills to discharge their duties to accord with these expectations (SWRB 2010). In these debates, the collective voices of social workers are absent. These yardsticks of professionalism have been developed almost entirely at the behest of governments, thus 'professionalism' as so understood has been externally imposed.

Organizationally, managers continue to exert greater control over *how* and *what* social workers do in their roles. In our experience of children's services, social workers are increasingly restricted to investigating reports of abuse or implementing Child Protection Plans, whereas the more direct work is done by support workers who are relatively less trained. Echoing our practice wisdom, Whittaker et al. conducted qualitative research in a northern England local authority children's centre accessed mostly by mothers, where 'parenting was compromised and children were deemed to have high levels of need' (2014: 481). The research was conducted with families who had multiple problems, including domestic violence and poverty, and were referred to the centre after assessments by social workers. Revealingly, one way by which the centre workers extracted some commitment from the parents was to 'threaten' to report them to their social workers if they did not adhere to the intervention plans, as reported in this participant testimony: 'They tell you what to do and threaten you with social workers and that you might lose your kids' (2014: 483). In this way, the social workers were cast not as partners who enabled families to change for the better, but as professionals who enforced a normative parenting approach. Although in this case the social workers were not doing therapeutic work with families to foster change, some parents modified their behaviour because of the risk of further enforcement action by social workers. The relationship-based work to foster change was conducted by other staff.

Similarly, in adult social care services, professional groups are often concerned about the high number of staff who do not have the title 'social worker' and believe that this might not lead to good outcomes for adults with complex needs (Godden 2012). Thus, one consequence of organizational professionalism is that the definitional space of social work has become more restricted. Another drawback is that the creative avenues of practice are closed off because of greater specification of work processes. Thus, there is decreasing professional autonomy and discretion in social work, highlighting again the explanatory power of the concept of organizational professionalism.

Research note: Conceptualizing 'de-professionalization'

Some writers argue that organizational professionalism is actually a form of 'de-professionalization'. Although those who take this view usually do not explain the term, when it is employed, there is the implicit assumption that greater professional autonomy is the same as professionalism (for instance, Rogowski 2011). By this interpretation, the greater freedom that social workers have in their role, the more professionalism they attain or display.

Reflection point 2.2

Healy and Meagher (2004) ascribe 'de-professionalization' three meanings: first, there is the 'fragmentation and routinisation of social work' (p. 244), in that social work is now broken down into small tasks, which have in turn been computerized; second, as we have described from our own professional experience, there is the increasing use of auxiliary social care staff in support roles previously discharged by their qualified counterparts; and third, according to Healy and Meagher, there is the reverse situation, whereby trained social workers are employed in organizations that do not make full use of their skills and qualifications.

While we acknowledge that it would appear that the current trend in Anglo-Saxon countries is a narrower scope of the social work role, we also believe that it may not all have entirely negative consequences. Some potential advantages that may arise from 'professionalism from without' are the following:

- It could lead to an elevated status for social work, thereby reducing its apparent inferiority *vis-à-vis* other professions. In court, complex assessments by social workers who have more knowledge of the family or service users have sometimes been set aside, and more work by 'experts' has been demanded (Munby 2013), even though they are less acquainted with the issues. Thus, one efficacy of professionalism would be that the 'professional judgement' of social workers would be accorded similar status to allied professions.
- It could result in social workers enjoying more discretion in their roles because their judgements would be accepted as equally valid as those of long-established professions.
- Politically, social workers may be better placed to advocate for service users, and for improvement in the conditions of the workforce.
- A more skilled workforce could mean better outcomes for service users. The evidence from research with older people is that they value social workers who are 'professional', skilled and knowledgeable (Manthorpe et al. 2008).

At this point, we would like you to reflect on whether professionalism must have a completely negative impact on social work, and how the profession can maintain its 'caring' and ethical value-base while attaining the requisite skill set.

Exercise 2.2: Debating the efficacy of professionalism in social work

In this chapter, we have provided an overview of professionalism. We conclude with a series of reflective questions regarding social work and professionalism:

- What role does a shared sense of professional identity have in uniting social work practitioners, especially those who might be working in very specialized or particular circumstances?
- Is the development of social work as a profession an unequivocal good and, if not, what might be problematic about this trend?
- Is it possible for social work to be a profession in a similar way to other public service professions (e.g. the medical or nursing professions), or is there something distinctive about what professionalism means for social work?
- How might an increased sense of professionalism lead to social work becoming more 'business-like'? What might be the positives and negatives of this process?

From reading this chapter, you will have seen that professionalism has brought certain gains to social work, including the support and solidarity that a shared professional identity can offer to social workers across a wide range of roles and settings. Perhaps you reflected on how far this is borne out in your own role or prospective future role. At the same time, your own experiences might either support or challenge the idea that the price of professionalizing social work is increased regulation.

Summary and conclusion

In this chapter, we have explored the nature of 'professionalism'. We have argued that its various derivations, such as 'profession' and 'professional', have powerful symbolic value in everyday language such that since the post-War period, various occupational groups have sought to be classified as 'professions'. Social work is no exception. Consequently, in the first part of this chapter we explored the origins of social work as a profession to historically situate current developments. The key message from our exposition is that unlike other occupations that seek the title of 'profession', social work has become subject to more regulation, perhaps because of its important role in the welfare state, which also makes it an intensely *political* profession. Thus, increasingly, when applied to social work, the term 'professionalism', from the theoretical viewpoint of discourse, refers to the legislation, regulations and knowledge that shape what practitioners should know, what they should do and how they should behave. However, it also has to be recognized that the profession of social work is also involved in *shaping* the discourse of professionalization. For example, through their collective activities, such as via professional organizations and academic bodies, social workers attempt to influence the government and the public about their unique professional skills. Hence, power is exerted both from outside and from within the profession to professionalize social work overall. While it could be argued that professionalization could lead to a more skilled workforce, the quest to instil professionalism in social work has resulted in less autonomy in practice because of increased statutory guidance from governments about social workers' role and duties, and there has been a reduced role for social work in statutory services. A skilled workforce may therefore come at a cost.

Professionalism as discourse, based on Foucault's work, places the responsibility on the individual and, in this way, echoes some of the themes in Evetts' professionalism 'from without' (Evetts 2003). The similarities are that the former appears to take the position that the individual's skill set must be elevated, but there is not as much resonance about the duty of the organization to nurture professional development. Additionally, the power relationship in both approaches is skewed in favour of the more powerful counterpart in the relationship; that is, either governments or employers because the latter can make laws and enact policies to propagate a particular (managerialist) conception of professionalism while the former (most local authorities) enforce and implement government agendas.

Towards the end of the chapter, we also discussed professionalism as culture. Theories of culture focus on the person–community interaction, highlighting the potential of the group to provide and nourish the identity of the individual.

Applied to social work, this refers to the shared understandings and values of the professional community. We believe therefore that professionalism as culture is a model more consistent with the quest to elevate the skill set of the workforce while also maintaining its ethical value-base and protecting social work from descending into an entirely rational–technical endeavour. Professionalism as culture also entails that members of the group have shared expectations. These include the ability to practise independently (with increasing experience), the capability to seek support and training to increase one's knowledge and skills, and the personal qualities to manage the complex emotions that arise within practice. In the literature, this is sometimes described as *self-management*, which we discuss in the next chapter.

Key points from this chapter

- Influenced by the sociological literature, we examined contemporary theorizations of professionalism and applied them to recent policy developments in social work in the UK.
- We showed that some writers consider professionalism to be a form of discourse. By this formulation, the concept is embedded in institutional practices as well as professional language and other social relations, which powerfully sustains it as a 'real' idea, one with practical import for social work. Through discourse, professionalism as an idea shapes how people think of themselves and even determines how they behave in their private lives away from work.
- We considered professionalism as culture. By this we mean that groups assigned this classification believe that they have shared views of the world and they have identified patterns of approaching their work. Professionalism as culture also implies that a group of professionals have a shared view of what their members can do. They are able to exercise independent judgement and seek ways to improve their skills and knowledge. This latter point is referred to as self-management, which we discuss in the next chapter.
- We discussed occupational and organizational professionalism: the former is usually initiated by the members themselves while the latter is imposed externally onto the group and is likely to lead to reduced professional autonomy. We concluded that professionalism in social work can be categorized as organizational but this need not be a wholly negative consequence. Some potential positives include: an elevated status for social workers, benefits to service users through increased expertise, and a more politically-active profession.

Recommended reading

Evetts, J. (2014) The concept of professionalism: professional work, professional practice and learning, in S. Billett, C. Harteis and H. Gruber (eds.) *International Handbook of Research in Professional and Practice-based Learning* (pp. 29–56). Dordrecht: Springer.

3 Self-management skills

Chapter overview

By the end of this chapter, you will:

- Understand the meaning of self-management as a prerequisite for professionalism
- Be able to explain that there are different dimensions of self-management – in social work, the focus tends to be on self-efficacy and emotional intelligence
- Be able to draw on self-efficacy and emotional intelligence in your Continuing Professional Development (CPD) and engagement with service users and colleagues
- Understand that self-efficacy and emotional intelligence are skills that can be improved through regular practice

Introduction

In this chapter, we will explore self-management, which, as we explained in the preceding chapter, is an important aspect of professionalism. We begin by describing the concept, which we will show is adopted from the healthcare literature but is relevant to current social work. We will note the underdevelopment of self-management theory in social work and we will focus on two concepts, self-efficacy and emotional intelligence, which are the two dimensions more widely applied in our discipline. We will explain the conceptual links between self-efficacy and emotional intelligence and provide illustrative practice examples.

What is self-management?

Self-management in social work is associated with self-efficacy, confidence, self-control and emotional intelligence. The concept originated in the healthcare literature, where it referred to the close involvement of patients in planning for their medical care in the community after hospitalization (de Silva 2011). This includes patients being trained by nurses and doctors to oversee their own care at home by, for example, using medical equipment, exercising regularly and adopting lifestyles conducive to good health. Another aspect of self-management is self-monitoring. Here, patients are taught to identify the point when their health begins to deteriorate, again so that they can inform professionals. You may, for instance, know that people diagnosed with diabetes are provided with equipment to test their glucose levels at home. If this exceeds the target, then they are expected to inform their health team for advice or alter their lifestyle, for instance by changing their diet to reduce the amount of glucose in their blood.

Therefore, intrinsic to the concept of self-management is a model of *collaboration* and *problem-solving*. Professionals and patients collaborate and form a partnership to assist the latter. The central idea is that health professionals train people in the most effective approaches to handling their own care needs while in hospital. After discharge, the patient assumes the responsibility for the daily control and monitoring of their condition. However, the purpose of the training is to facilitate identification of problems from the perspective of the patient (Lorig and Holman 2003). Thus, professionals assist patients to resolve issues that are problematic to them, instead of having care plans imposed on them without collaborative consultation. This is because the assumption is that healthcare interventions are more likely to succeed if patients take as much ownership as possible of the implementation of their care plans. Advocates of self-management would argue that if people are not closely involved in developing strategies to meet their needs, the plans will be ineffective because they will lack self-motivation to maintain them. Thus, the success of self-management plans is dependent on people's *motivation* and *capacity* to follow plans developed with professionals.

Developed within healthcare, self-management is now widely applied beyond medical interventions and has been used, for instance, to explain behaviour in schools and the workplace (Blok 2017). In the management literature, self-management has been adopted within the context of employees' self-reliance and ability to take responsibility for their conduct, and act with minimal direction from managers (Uhl-Bien and Graen 1998). It is in this latter sense that we adopt self-management in this chapter because it has resonance for social work practice in terms of professionalism and ethics. Self-management implies that in order to conform to the professional title 'social worker', one needs to be motivated to adhere to the highest practice standards. These include maintaining appropriate relationships with service users, displaying the correct emotional responses to practice situations, having high standards of communication, and even meeting 'everyday' social norms such as politeness, time-keeping and respect for others. Self-management is also applied in management studies to refer to the ability of teams to be semi-autonomous and organized to maintain their own internal processes to achieve goals (Langfred 2007). In this latter respect, the concept is applicable to social workers adopting the group supervision model as a problem-solving technique or providing emotional support to each other. Furthermore, the central idea in self-management, that patients should share the responsibility for their own care, applies to CPD and career planning. By this interpretation, professionals are obliged to reflect on their skills and seek regular training to improve their practice. In this way, practitioners keep abreast of the latest developments in the field, including knowledge of the interventions that achieve the best outcomes for service users (BASW 2012a) — practitioners adopt evidence-informed approaches (see McLaughlin and Teater 2017).

Turning the discussion to engagement with service users, self-management in social work means that ethical practice is that which seeks to involve service users wherever possible. Consequently, we have an ethical duty to encourage service users' participation in interventions in order to enable them to find their own solutions to their own difficulties.

Types of self-management

In an analysis of the conceptual literature, Ryan and Swain (2009) showed that there are different understandings of the term, based on disciplinary perspectives. Self-management can refer to processes, programmes or outcomes:

- **Processes** of self-management refer to the skills that people have (or ought to have) to engage in successful self-management. Examples include goal-setting, decision-making and self-evaluation skills. In a review of the interdisciplinary literature on self-management, Blok (2017) also suggested that psychological and cognitive skills such as self-efficacy, motivation and perseverance are important.
- **Programmes** of self-management are the specific interventions or training that professionals provide to service users (or patients) to enable them to assume control of their condition. In terms of professionalism, this refers to CPD programmes, courses and training provided by employers for social workers to enhance their skills.
- Lastly, **outcomes** of self-management pertain to the goals of the programmes – for instance, if a social worker is trained in court skills, the aim is to improve the quality of their reports, their verbal communication when giving evidence and their understanding of the law.

In this chapter, we are concerned with **processes** because we want to highlight the skills professionals require to self-manage their work. We also want to show that the skills are necessary for good social work in terms of achieving the best outcomes for service users. We take the view that even from the perspective of *interventions*, it is conceivable that they are more likely to be successful if a service user has these skills.

We can use the hypothetical situation of Jessica, a girl subject to a Child Protection Plan (CPP). In England, a CPP is established by a group of professionals when it is judged that a child is at risk of significant harm. The aim of a CPP is to reduce the identified risks and, concomitantly, decrease the need for further professional input in the care of the child. As part of the CPP intervention, Jessica's parents are assisted to develop the following skills: how to prioritize Jessica's needs, how to resolve problems on their own early to prevent escalation and how to manage their time to attend specialist appointments for Jessica. In this scenario, arguably, the risks to Jessica are likely to diminish after the implementation of the CPP. This contrasts with children whose parents do not have these skills. It is for this reason that we later discuss the skills for supporting people to change and self-manage (see Chapter 5).

The case of Mrs Jones and the 'de-skilling' that can occur from complex cases may be familiar to social workers. It is important to conduct a skills audit by

Exercise 3.1: Reflecting on our skills

As a Newly-Qualified Social Worker (NQSW) in a dementia team, you are assigned to work with Mrs Jones who has two daughters, Martha and Aimee. The children referred their mother for social work assessment because they feared that she was unable to live independently – she was not eating regularly, her bills remained unpaid and she was not claiming all of her welfare benefits. They were also concerned that she was 'lonely' and that this was affecting her mental health. When you visited Mrs Jones, you realized that she communicated using sign language. As a NQSW, you found this to be a complex case because of the multiple factors that had to be considered in the assessment. You also found that there were gaps in your knowledge about welfare benefits to which Mrs Jones was entitled, how to meet her communication needs and legal frameworks for assessing her.

- Drawing on the preceding discussion of self-management, explain how you will address these gaps in your skills and knowledge.

reflecting honestly on our current capabilities and the aspect(s) of our practice that we need to improve upon (Wilkins and Boahen 2013). We should then plan the training required and, equally importantly, keep records of those who attended.

Up to this point we have explained that there is a long-standing tradition of debate over the meaning of self-management in healthcare, alongside a good body of applied research. However, the social work literature on the links with professionalism is less developed. Instead of the broad category 'self-management', when applied to professional practice and conduct, social work researchers explore the discrete dimensions of self-management such as self-efficacy and emotional intelligence.

Self-management in social work

The aim of this section is to apply the theoretical explorations of self-management in the healthcare literature to social work. Recall that in the earlier discussion, we highlighted that self-management in healthcare involves the active participation of patients in their medical care. The concept of self-management is therefore consistent with the social work values of self-determination and co-production because it entails the ethical position that service users have a right to be involved in decision-making about their care. It follows from this assumption that interventions in which service users are closely involved are more ethically sound, as far as the values of social work extend, than those in which care plans are imposed on them.

The reference to partnership between professionals and patients in the management of long-term conditions also draws attention to the quest in social work to equalize the power between service users and practitioners by considering the former as 'experts' in their own right (McLaughlin 2009). The corollary of this is that, in social work, it is accepted that practitioners have an ethical responsibility to include service users in decisions about their care. We discuss this aspect of self-management, where professionals enable others to oversee their care, in Chapter 5.

However, self-management is also applicable to how professionals oversee their own work (we discuss this further in Chapter 4). In this chapter, we also want to show the conceptual overlap between self-management and professionalism. One strand of this formulation refers to professional conduct in everyday interaction with colleagues and service users. Writing from this standpoint, Thompson (2016) identifies the following psychological and personal characteristics:

- **Self-awareness:** How I am affecting a given situation and how it is also impacting on me.
- **Emotional intelligence:** Understanding other people's emotions as well as my own. This also includes awareness of certain situations that trigger specific feelings in me.
- **Relationality:** Recognizing myself as a possible tool in changing service users' situations.
- **Self-empowerment:** Developing skills to cope with the demands of the profession, where reasonable.

Another strand of self-management, this one in relation to professional standards, is about the need for social workers to seek opportunities for training and systematize plans to further their knowledge and practice (NASW 2012). This might include, for instance, attending training regularly and documenting these in your records, keeping abreast of policy changes to understand their impact on service users, researching about effective interventions and treatment for clients, and reflecting on your skills. In this formulation, self-management is similar to CPD. In most countries, social workers are required to undertake CPD to maintain their professional titles (BASW 2012a; HCPC 2017). However, the onus on *ownership* in self-management shifts this to the terrain of ethics, by which we mean that it implies an ethical duty on professionals to be responsible for updating their knowledge and skills, where possible. Thus, similar to the earlier discussion about patients taking responsibility for their own care, self-management is applicable to taking ownership of our career development as social workers.

Blok (2017) examined self-management behaviour (SMB) by reviewing the interdisciplinary literature to identify the pre-existing personal qualities and circumstances that are required for 'good' SMB. Blok termed these 'antecedents' and suggested that they could be classified as 'psychological characteristics', 'received support', 'collaboration', 'socio-economic and cultural characteristics', 'obstacles' and 'physical characteristics' (2017: 141–142). Although Blok's work was about SMB in patients, we discuss it here because it has implications for professionalism. In noting that individual psychology is important for SMB, Blok found that the most relevant psychological attribute is self-efficacy.

Psychological characteristics of SMB (Blok 2017: 142)

- Self-efficacy
- Acceptance, mindfulness and other skills
- Motivation/goal desire
- Psychosocial functioning/development
- Personal characteristics
- Perceptions of cause/importance of disease
- Cognitive ability, prioritization and problem-solving skills
- Coping skills, coping planning, proactive personality, perseverance and attitude

Having outlined the analytic thread between self-management and professionalism, we now discuss self-efficacy and emotional intelligence, which are the two elements of self-management widely discussed in the social work literature.

Self-efficacy and social work

Self-efficacy theory is credited to the work of Albert Bandura, who defined it as:

> . . . people's beliefs about their capabilities to produce designated levels of performance that exercise influence over events that affect their lives. Self-efficacy beliefs determine how people feel, think, motivate themselves and behave. Such beliefs produce these diverse effects through four major processes. They include cognitive, motivational, affective and selection processes.
>
> (Bandura 1994)

Bandura's theorization is about people's confidence that they have the ability to shape their life circumstances. In Bandura's work, some aspects of self-efficacy are innate – for instance, some people have naturally high self-confidence. However, according to Bandura, our self-efficacy can grow the more we overcome what we initially perceive as difficult challenges. Bandura termed this aspect of his theory 'self-mastery' – that is, the more skilled we are at a particular task, the more confidence we develop in our ability to fulfil it. Bandura also postulated that self-efficacy can be gained through *modelling*. We can observe the achievements of other people who face similar situations and learn the skills that they deploy to overcome their challenges. Through observation of, and learning from, successful people, we too can develop confidence in our abilities. In addition to observing and learning from others, Bandura argued that we can gain self-efficacy through *persuasion*. By this it is meant that we can convince or be coaxed by others into believing that we can accomplish a given task. One interpretation of Bandura's model is that as we succeed in discharging complex tasks, our (self) confidence grows, which in turn motivates us to attempt more difficult assignments, with the potential to increase our self-efficacy further.

Explaining the links: self-management, self-efficacy and social work

- In order for professionals to engage in successful self-management, they need to have the confidence to identify gaps in their skills. They also require self-motivation to attend training or CPD and implement new skills regularly in practice. This is referred to as 'self-efficacy'.
- We have argued that self-efficacy also applies to how social workers plan their careers to gain the skills and knowledge for safe and effective practice (BASW 2012a).
- If social workers are confident, they can try out new and creative interventions with service users. They can also attempt to resolve service users' complex problems because they more readily believe that they have the requisite skills and knowledge to do so.
- If social workers are motivated, they will conduct themselves according to the highest ethical and professional standards.

It can be seen from the previous discussion that Bandura's theorization emphasizes *individual* psychology. This is because Bandura's model refers to a person's 'innate' mental abilities. For instance, even if other people can motivate and convince us that we are very good at something, at the base level, we ourselves need to believe that this is the case. We can use the case of Usain Bolt, who holds the world-record in the 100 metres sprint race, as an illustration. We can imagine that before he broke the record, Bolt's coaches would have impressed on him that he was capable of doing it; however, he too needed to have the confidence in his own abilities before attempting the feat. Similarly, there are times when we find the internal resources to motivate ourselves and persevere with a task with which we initially struggled in the absence of external motivating factors.

However, it has also been argued that social factors can impact on our self-efficacy. Blok (2017) suggests that some of these might include the resources in the community, our own social circumstances and our financial situations.

Furthermore, social work research has questioned the link between self-mastery and self-efficacy developed by Bandura. While some studies report that the more skilful practitioners are, the more confident they are in their abilities, some research has not identified this link (see Tompsett et al. [2017] for a discussion of the literature). Instead, confidence may depend on how professionals manage their emotional states, their abilities to apply formal and practical knowledge to similar situations, and their 'relational skills' (Bogo et al. 2017). In their study of practitioners and qualifying social workers, Bogo and her colleagues found that those who described themselves as confident also claimed to be calm when faced with challenging cases. This attitude enabled the professionals to draw on their previous knowledge in managing difficult cases. Interestingly, in the study, both confidence and a lack thereof were associated with anxiety; however, social workers who *self-described* as confident remained calm, even though they were anxious, because they had mastered the ability to regulate their emotions. These 'confident' workers were also conscious of clients' emotional states while not allowing this to materially affect their own feelings and judgements.

Summary

- There are different definitions of self-management; however, there is a consensus that self-efficacy is intrinsic to the concept.
- In the work and theorization of Bandura, it is claimed that self-efficacy is innate but can also be gained from observing our peers and their skills and from receiving positive feedback for our work.

In the social work literature, due to the importance ascribed to self-efficacy, researchers have sought to 'measure' it and to explore how professionals can gain or develop the skill. We discuss one of these studies below.

Research note: 'Measuring' self-efficacy in NQSWs

Research by Carpenter (2015) was designed to measure the self-efficacy of NQSWs. The NQSWs were asked to complete a survey that included a tool to measure their self-efficacy at the start of a one-year post-qualifying programme, three months into the programme and again at the end of the first year. This study is significant and often cited in the social work literature on self-efficacy because of the large number of participants – 2,000 NQSWs – and because data was collected over an extended period. A selection of the findings is presented here.

- Although participants were confident at the start of the study, their confidence reduced at three months but increased again towards the end of the NQSW programme. The authors suggest that at the three month point, participants became more aware of the challenges of their role, and therefore felt less confident in their abilities than they envisaged.
- Self-efficacy was associated with clarity about the role – the more certain NQSWs were about their job, the greater their self-efficacy. Simultaneously, NQSWs who reported high self-efficacy also reported high role conflict. The researchers hypothesized that these NQSWs were more likely to be involved in complex cases, bringing them into contact with complex organizational structures and budgetary limitations. Unsurprisingly, it was also found that self-efficacy was positively linked to intrinsic job satisfaction.

Carpenter and colleagues' research evidenced the multi-faceted nature of self-efficacy. The research suggests that self-efficacy can be negatively affected by a *realization* of the complexity of a task, even when we have not attempted it.

The research also supports the self-mastery thesis by Bandura: as we gather a portfolio of success, we become more confident in our abilities. Thus, on a practical level, self-efficacy can develop from simply trying! This also indicates that self-efficacy is a *skill* because it can be improved through practice.

The research by Bogo and Carpenter suggests that our belief in our capabilities is linked to our capacity to manage the emotional dimensions of practice. In the former's study, self-confidence was associated with the ability to remain calm, while in the latter's, awareness of the complexity of a task made some professionals doubt their ability to fulfil it. Therefore, our level of performance is not only about our skill set but also about how we manage the emotions associated with our role. This is a key dimension of the concept of emotional intelligence.

Emotional intelligence and social work

The concept of emotional intelligence is credited to the work of Salovey and Mayer (1990). Traditionally, researchers distinguished between reason and emotion: the former was ascribed to cognitive processes such as analysing and deliberating and the latter to feelings such as happiness and anxiety. In this formulation, feelings (or emotions) are viewed pejoratively as likely to interfere with reasoning. This understanding continues to prevail in everyday life. We have all probably been advised at some point by friends or relatives to 'keep our emotions in check', or something similar. The inference here is that once we 'control' our emotions, our reasoning can do the 'proper' work of making decisions or analysing the situation. However, Salovey and Mayer argued that emotion is an important dimension of intelligence, especially the kind that enables us to attune to other people's feelings. They conceptualized this as emotional intelligence:

> . . . *the ability to monitor one's own and others' feelings and emotions, to discriminate among them and to use this information to guide one's thinking and actions* . . . It focuses [on] the recognition and use of one's own and others' emotional states to solve problems and regulate behaviour.
>
> (Salovey and Mayer 1990: 190; emphasis in original)

Notice that, from this definition, one purpose of recognizing our emotions and other people's feelings is to problem-solve. Therefore, in the professional context, being emotional in the everyday sense does not conform to emotional intelligence unless one can reflect on the emotions, categorize them and draw upon them to find solutions. In this respect, emotional intelligence can also be considered a prerequisite for decision-making and analysis (Wilkins and Boahen 2013). Furthermore, emotional intelligence entails the *interpersonal* (acknowledging and appreciating other people's emotions and how this is impacting on them) and *intrapersonal* (possessing the same capacity to understand our own feelings and their effect on our actions and decisions). Another point of note is that emotional intelligence is not considered to be a solely natural or inborn ability that distinct groups of people have – it is argued that it is also possible to *learn* the personality traits conducive to emotional intelligence (Singh 2006).

The personality traits of emotional intelligence

Emotional intelligence is an important skill for social workers because service users often have painful life experiences, which they can express through different emotions. For instance, some service users may distrust professionals because they have power that is not always exercised in their best interests (Tew 2006). Other service users may be angry at their adverse life situation, while others may have encountered loss and bereavement and thereby feel disenfranchised. Therefore, in order to assist service users, social workers need to *understand and express* a range of emotions (Morrison 2007).

There is a decent body of literature on emotional intelligence in social work, including how social workers understand it and the emotions conducive to good practice within an emotional intelligence framework. We discussed some of these personality traits in Table 3.1 and will now draw on this in the next exercise.

Exercise 3.2: Engaging with emotions in practice

This exercise is designed to assist you to reflect on how we can engage with our emotions in practice to enact change. To achieve this we would like you too draw on the ideas in Table 3.1 to reflect on how your feelings can guide you in your work with service users and patients.

In this scenario, you are the social worker on duty in a local authority children's safeguarding team. You are called to the reception to speak to a 30-year-old woman called Tulela who wants to make a self-referral. Tulela came to the UK from Namibia as a student five years ago, accompanied by her partner and two children. However, she could not continue her studies in the UK because her parents who funded her both died in a car accident. As Tulela did not continue her studies, she does not have the right to stay in the UK. Consequently, she is now an undocumented migrant. During your conversation with Tulela, she tells you that she and her children live in one room in a 'shared house', which she rents after fleeing domestic abuse by her partner. Tulela works on night shifts in a hospital. During this time, the children stay with her friend, she collects them after work and takes them home.

- Reflect on and list your emotions about Tulela and her children's situation. Can you explain the sources of your feelings about the case? How can your emotions affect your practice in this case? Drawing on Table 3.1, consider the advantages and disadvantages of drawing on your emotions to guide your actions.

Table 3.1 Emotional Intelligence Framework

Emotional intelligence personality trait	Commentary
Self-awareness (Ingram 2013)	This is the understanding that sometimes our presence alone can generate anxieties in service users because of the power inherent in the professional title, 'social worker'. We should also be aware that, however unwittingly, we can have negative and positive impacts on colleagues, fellow professionals and service users. Thus, to demonstrate professional self-awareness, we need good observation and analytical skills – first, to perceive that we act differently to some people and, concomitantly, other individuals behave differently towards us; and second, as professionals, we need to analyse the reasons why this occurs.
Motivation (Rogers et al. 2017)	This is linked to self-efficacy because we may be more motivated to approach a task if we feel confident that we have the requisite skills. On the other hand, feeling that we are powerless to change a situation may negatively impact on our motivation.
Emotional control (Kinman and Grant 2011)	This refers to our ability to prevent our negative emotions from overwhelming us. Without this, we may feel powerless and incapable. Uncontrolled emotions can also cause fear or dislike of certain service users.
Empathy (Ingram 2013)	This is required in all aspects of social work practice: from our first engagement with service users, to planning interventions, reviews and ending our involvement in cases. Empathy is an appreciation of how people's difficult life situations have impacted upon them. If we are empathetic, we do not blame service users for causing their situation or being unable to immediately change it.
Showing 'insight' into one's emotional state and ability to 'articulate' and 'name' our emotions (Grant et al. 2014)	In a professional sense, we demonstrate this when we feel safe that our managers will not judge us negatively. Similar to reflection and self-awareness, we demonstrate insight by recognizing our present emotions, how they are impacting on our work and others, and our limitations.
Ability to reflect (McFadden et al. 2015; see also D'Cruz et al. 2007 for a conceptual analysis)	Reflection is a core social work skill. In the emotional intelligence sense, it refers to the capacity to think about how life events have shaped service users. It also refers to our capacity to examine how our own history of trauma affects our professional conduct, decision-making and motivation.
'Tuning in' to the service users' needs (Stone 2016)	This is similar to self-awareness, reflection and empathy. When we 'tune in', we attempt to understand service users' situations better and develop a fuller appreciation of their current emotional state.

Reflection point 3.1

The scenario about Tulela and her two children is likely to generate a range of emotions in any practitioner. Tulela has experienced bereavement and loss as a result of her parents' deaths. This is likely to be accentuated by her inability to attend the funeral because, as an undocumented migrant, she would not have the requisite immigration papers to travel. Compounding these losses, she has also been abused by her partner – this is likely to make some of us angry at the children's father for his oppression of a very vulnerable person. We may also feel profound empathy for Tulela, and we may be very concerned with, and worried about, her children's welfare.

Advocates of emotional intelligence would postulate that these emotions should be drawn upon constructively to *change* the family's situation for the better. As a social worker, you can also draw on the Framework in Table 3.1 and identify the skills conducive to changing the lives of Tulela and her children. The oppression by her partner may anger you but you need to demonstrate 'insight' into your emotional state, and self-awareness about how anger affects you, in order to deploy these feelings in a professional way to empower Tulela. For instance, if you know that when you are angry you are liable to shout at people, then you require emotional control.

However, the feeling of anger could also motivate you in the work or you may feel more empathetic, thereby reassuring Tulela that you are an ally who will work alongside her.

- *In consultation with Table 3.1, identify the emotions that you will draw upon in this work.*

Summary and conclusion

In this chapter, we have discussed self-management, drawing on the management, medicine and healthcare. This is because we find them more developed than in the social work literature. We began by explaining that self-management in the healthcare literature as they have a more developed research tradition in these topics than social work is about the participation and involvement of patients in the drawing up of their care plans by professionals. Central to the concept is that professionals actively encourage patients' involvement and they do the work *with* them. On their part, patients assume responsibility for implementing the plans at home. The debates about self-management turn on whether it is a *process* involving skills and, if so, what they are; whether it is about *programmes*; or whether it is about *outcomes*. We have shown that, increasingly, self-management is now applied to social work. In our field, it refers to professionals assuming responsibility for the highest standards of practice, including CPD, and a recognition that ethical practice entails the involvement of service users in all interventions. Throughout the discussion, we emphasized that self-management includes *individual* psychological factors such as motivation, self-efficacy and emotional intelligence. In social work, the literature on self-efficacy and emotional intelligence is relatively well developed – research focuses on traits instead of the broad conceptual framework. To maintain this disciplinary tradition, we explored self-efficacy and emotional intelligence. This chapter has shown that being a 'good' social worker is not only about having technical skills, but also having the ability to manage and cultivate the psychological aspects of the profession.

Key points from this chapter

- We explained that self-management in the healthcare literature refers to strategies by professionals to involve patients in planning their care after discharge. Patients and medical staff jointly draw up the care plan with the intention that the service user takes ownership and responsibility going forward.
- Self-management is associated with psychological skills and personality traits such as self-efficacy, motivation, emotional intelligence and perseverance.
- Self-management is gaining attention in social work because it is consistent with the values of self-determination and anti-oppressive practice.
- Increasingly, self-management is applied to social workers' obligation to enhance their skills and knowledge through CPD.
- Through the discussion of emotional intelligence, we showed that self-management is about the ability to manage the emotional demands of social work.

Recommended reading

Blok, A.C. (2017) A middle-range explanatory theory of self-management behavior for collaborative research and practice, *Nursing Forum*, 52 (2): 138–146.

Morrison, T. (2007) Emotional intelligence, emotion and social work: context, characteristics, complications and contribution, *British Journal of Social Work*, 37 (2): 245–263.

Wilkins, D. and Boahen, G. (2013) *Critical Analysis Skills for Social Workers* (Chapter 3). Maidenhead: Open University Press.

4 Identifying skills for professionalism

Chapter overview

By the end of this chapter, you will:

- Be able to recognize the key elements that need to be in place to support professionalism in all aspects of social work practice
- Understand how these elements interact in everyday practice
- Know how to identify practical examples of how you can exercise professionalism

Introduction

This chapter explores the hallmarks of professionalism that routinely feature across all aspects of social work practice. This will enable you, as you read the next four chapters on specific skills, to answer the question, 'What makes this area of practice "professional"?'. We argue that professionalism entails being able to increasingly integrate and develop all the areas of competence that you demonstrated as a successful social work student.

Social workers in the UK have become familiar with frameworks of professional standards that state what social workers should be able to do in relation to a particular role or set of tasks, such as assessing people's needs, care planning, working with families or presenting a court report. Some standards (for example, England's Knowledge and Skills Statements for working with children or adults) are subdivided to reflect what is expected at different levels of career development. Standards thus provide a way of measuring how well a practitioner's competence matches up to an externally-set expectation. In this book, our approach to skills is more akin to the concept of *capabilities*. Capabilities refer to a holistic integration of personal qualities, values, knowledge and understanding, as well as practical skills. The concept is also developmental, in the sense that a person's capabilities continuously adapt to new and changing contexts; thus, there is a built-in expectation of reflective practice and continuous learning (Biggs and Tang 2007; Cooper 2008).

In the next four chapters, we focus on areas of skill that are important for autonomous professional practice across all social work roles: self-management, communication, risk and safeguarding, and leadership. These four areas are best thought of as 'organizing themes' for thinking in a holistic way about professional

skills. Self-management, for example, involves many discrete areas of ability, such as being alert to professional standards and conduct, or being proactive in one's own development. These abilities are also needed for successful communication, managing risk and safeguarding. Similarly, being a proficient communicator involves skills and techniques that form the heart of effective leadership and safeguarding.

We argue that professionalism can be present in all aspects of routine, everyday social work. Where it exists, it is rather like the lettering that runs through a stick of rock. Working 'professionally' involves having a sound knowledge of, and ability in, key aspects of social work, and then being able to integrate these in everyday practice. Of course, social workers don't usually do this integration consciously. However, becoming aware of the different elements and how they are being integrated is a key part of professional learning. We suggest that there are eight key elements that need to be in place to support professionalism in the areas of self-management, communication, risk and safeguarding, and leadership. These are:

- Self-awareness about professional and personal values
- Appropriate and ethical use of professional power
- Critical analysis
- Research mindedness
- Emotional resilience
- A sense of professional identity
- Engaging actively in supervision
- Continuing Professional Development

Self-awareness about professional and personal values

There is no definitive blueprint for the values held by social work practitioners: regulatory codes of conduct co-exist alongside detailed statements and guidance published by professional bodies. The BASW Code of Ethics for Social Work (2014) describes social work values in terms of a commitment to achieving social justice, human rights and professional integrity, thus incorporating the international definition and principles of the profession (IFSW 2014). It goes on to offer general ethical principles to guide social workers' practice in accordance with the values, which relate to the behaviour, character, responsibilities and relationships expected of a professional practitioner. There can be tensions in articulating professional values because to some extent they are open to interpretation – they also interact with an individual's own religious, moral, cultural, political and ideological beliefs (Doel et al., 2009; Banks 2012). For example, most social workers probably concur with some ideal of social justice, yet this is a contested concept (Thompson 2017), and individuals likely hold a variety of political stances on what a just society looks like and how it can be achieved. Consider, for instance, the controversial requirement that social workers carry out age assessments of unaccompanied asylum-seeking children and report this to the Home Office. Social workers are being directed by central government policy to treat these children differently to other children (Gower 2011), which goes against social work values and aims. How is it possible to uphold professional principles while adhering to the constraints of immigration law? Practitioners equally committed to social justice might deal with this dilemma differently. One response would be to mitigate this statutory duty by advocating for the individual child as much as possible, supporting them to obtain appropriate services. Another practitioner might engage in political action (a campaigning group such as Social Work Action Network or a trade union) aimed at reforming immigration policies.

How do values contribute to social workers' professionalism? One example is to provide a source of reflection and support when making difficult decisions. Social workers learn to acknowledge their own personal values and beliefs, and then must reconcile these with *professional* values. When social work evokes difficult feelings, drawing on professional values can support practitioners in managing these. For example, an experienced forensic social worker in a mental health hospital suggests that, when working with service users who have committed very serious and harmful offences, it is important to avoid labelling them (Hebb 2013). Thus, when assessing risk, or evaluating how well a person has reponded to a treatment or care plan, understanding the person's unique life history provides the impetus to explore and develop their strengths. This kind of self-questioning and emotional self-management can be difficult and painful. Akhtar (2013) argues, however, that social workers' ability to balance personal and professional values continues to develop alongside other aspects of their professional competence, meaning that this balancing act may ease with time.

Practice dilemmas may also arise when trying to respond ethically to people's situations and needs within organizational and financial parameters (Whittington 2006; Banks 2012). Holding fast to social work values can help practitioners have the professional confidence to adopt a questioning stance rather than taking structural inequalities for granted (Smith 2008). It may not always be possible to change a decision, and still less an institutional response, but more modest actions such as reframing the way a problem is perceived, articulating the service user's perspective or proposing alternative plans can be realistic ways of working within a value-based approach (Smith 2008). In this regard, social work values contribute to a sense of professional identity and provide a supportive reference point, especially when faced with challenges on a personal, organizational or political level.

Reflection point 4.1

It is highly likely that you have experienced dilemmas relating to your own professional and personal values. Think of an example from your working life when you were torn between opposing courses of action that would have an impact on someone's care.

- *Why did you find this difficult?*
- *Which values underpinned the conflicting decisions?*

Examples from other practitioners include:

- Having to reduce people's care services on budgetary grounds, knowing that this will impact negatively on their opportunities for socializing.
- Deciding whether to join industrial strike action against job losses that will have a future impact on service users' lives.

Appropriate and ethical use of professional power

Service users rightly perceive social workers as having a great deal of power, but research suggests that social workers may feel their own autonomy to be limited by agency, statutory, procedural and budgetary constraints (Jones 2001; Dumbrill 2006). Objectively, professional power is most overt when social workers recommend interventions such as Child Protection Plans or compulsory mental health admissions. Even when the service is intended to be enabling, social workers typically carry out gatekeeping activities, such as an assessment of needs, which may result in people being deemed ineligible to receive the type or level of service they want. Regardless of the nature of the intervention, social workers continually use their professional power to make decisions in the context of competing interests and perspectives, for example when balancing the needs of a service user and carer, or weighing an adult's autonomy against organizational or restrictive definitions of risk.

Clearly, professionals need to ensure that they do not abuse their power. An obvious example is being careful not to overstep professional boundaries set out in ethical codes. Equally important examples include the unthinking use of exclusionary language (considered in Chapter 6) or regularly keeping service users waiting by arriving late for appointments (Smith 2008). Social workers can also use their professional power in an *enabling* way, such as when advocating on behalf of a service user. This will be most effective when they are able to call on up-to-date professional expertise, such as a sound knowledge of social work law, child and adult development, and research evidence about best practice – all of which lend weight to professional judgement. One illustration is an Approved Mental Health Professional's (AMHP) use of their professional power to bring a social perspective to a Mental Health Act assessment, perhaps being able to suggest appropriate actions and solutions that avoid admitting a person to hospital against their wishes (Matthews 2015).

At times, even for an experienced practitioner, exercising authority feels at odds with social work values, which emphasize empowering and supporting people to be heard and fulfil their potential. Social workers may need to place their own professional judgement over the service user's perspective when there is evidence of serious risk and harm. There can also be circumstances – rooted in social and cultural difference, unresolved psychological factors or a lack of agency support – in which social workers feel neither confident nor powerful, and in some situations they may also feel scared. This is where good quality supervision is important, offering safety, guidance and support to share decision-making and explore personal feelings about social work authority, including the obstacles and constraints that make this difficult.

Exercise 4.1: Exercising professional power

Consider the instances described previously of when social workers are called on to exercise professional power, such as making a decision about risk. Note a similar or different example from your own practice or studies. This will help you consider your personal stance on power, and identify areas where you need support from colleagues or in supervision.

Critical analysis

In this book, we use the term 'critical analysis' to mean examining the different elements of an issue to gain a deeper understanding, and using this understanding to inform social work intervention (Wilkins and Boahen 2013). It involves setting aside time to engage in a dialogue with oneself by thinking or writing, or a dialogue with colleagues and supervisors (Stokes and Schmidt 2012). Critical analysis – also referred to as critical thinking or critical reflection – requires practitioners to adopt an open-minded and questioning approach to the issues and circumstances that they encounter. This involves the ability to stand back and mobilize a wide range of knowledge – theories, research findings, practice knowledge, law and policy, and people's different perspectives – to gain insight into the whole picture. Criticality also implies drawing on professional values to make sense of knowledge. For example, some authors emphasize the importance of considering power relationships, which has relevance for our earlier discussion of Foucault (Glaister 2008; Fook 2015). This offers an opportunity to consider how social structures can contribute to an individual's problems or distress, and greater awareness can lead to more nuanced and creative solutions, even when it cannot directly challenge those structures (Miller 2005; Thompson 2017).

Critical reflection is not always easy. It can be very uncomfortable to realize that your initial view of a situation was not the right one (Munro 1999). More challenging still, Fook and Askeland (2006) suggest that it is important to consider your position in relation to inequality and your own part in maintaining potentially oppressive structures. Doing this can be unsettling and may raise personal dilemmas and conflicts. Critical reflection – whether with colleagues or in professional supervision – takes courage and requires safe opportunities to share ideas, thoughts and feelings.

Exercise 4.2: Opportunities for critical reflection and analysis

Make a list of your opportunities for standing back to critically analyse your practice, or imagine where these might arise in your future practice. Note where you feel these could be enhanced. Unless critical reflection is built into your role, for example as a student, it can be difficult to make time and space in a busy team. Critical analysis is, however, a vital professional skill rather than an optional luxury.

Despite its challenges, critical analysis is an essential prerequisite for decision-making in social work. The ability to question generalized assumptions and seek evidence is thought to equip social workers to handle uncertainty and complexity, avoid bias in making decisions, and to feel more confident about evidencing their thinking. Fook and others (2000) suggest that this ability develops over time: whereas new practitioners are more likely to stick to established procedures, expert social workers are likely to be critically reflective. On the other hand, literature reviews (for example, Turney 2014) suggest that social workers do not always use this skill sufficiently. (In Chapter 7, we explore two examples of analytical frameworks that have been developed to support the thinking process).

Research mindedness

Closely related to critical analysis, research mindedness involves understanding how to search for, critically evaluate and select relevant research to inform practice and enhance outcomes for service users. These are increasingly emphasized as broad skills that social workers need in their professional repertoire. Croisdale-Appleby (2014), in his review of social work education, argued that, alongside their other professional skills, social workers should be social scientists. By this he meant adopting a curious and analytical approach to the practice of social work by selecting and applying the most appropriate principles, methods and knowledge, as well as developing social work through gathering evidence and conducting practice-based research. In a similar vein, Orme and Shemmings (2010) suggest that social workers should have the skills to carry out small-scale research as part of their professional capability.

Reflection point 4.2

Although it is beyond the scope of this book to consider skills in doing research (consider Aveyard [2018] for more on this), look out for examples of where we draw attention to research evidence about what makes for effective professional skills and expertise. Familiarity with such studies will help you to develop your research mindedness.

Application to skills

What are the benefits of using research in practice? One argument is that openness to a range of evidence avoids reliance on a procedural approach (Romeo 2014). Weighing up research evidence can help practitioners view a situation from a new angle, providing the impetus to try a fresh approach when faced with an impasse or dilemma.

Research findings can also assist social workers when making complex decisions. Arguing for service developments can be more persuasive when supported by research evidence of the benefits for people who use services. At the same time, it is essential for practitioners to exercise professional judgement and take a critical approach to research findings. This is assisted by having an appreciation of the methods used to obtain research evidence, and the ability to interpret conflicting findings and recognize one's limitations. This may mean undertaking professional development, such as individual reading, peer learning, or attending external events and training. Organizations such as the Social Care Institute for Excellence (SCIE), The Institute for Research and Innovation in Social Services (Iriss) and the Joseph Rowntree Foundation (JRF) produce summaries of research findings, which can help busy social workers to balance research mindedness with other day-to-day priorities.

Emotional resilience

Regulatory and professional standards expect social workers to take responsibility for their own emotional resilience: the ability to constructively protect oneself, and bounce back, from adversity. Having emotional resilience is a mark of professionalism in that feeling overwhelmed with high levels of stress impacts negatively on the service, as well as being debilitating for the social worker. According to the 2015–16 Labour Force Survey (HSE 2016), health and social care professionals experience one of the highest rates of work-related stress in Britain. This may not surprise you because, although social work is generally a rewarding job, it is emotionally challenging. Concerns about workforce retention and burnout have prompted research studies to explore how emotional resilience can be supported (Collins 2007, 2008; Grant and Kinman 2012; Beddoe et al. 2013).

There are times when social workers need to conceal their immediate emotional response to maintain a non-judgemental or authoritative stance (Kinman et al. 2011); this is called 'emotional labour', and it can become stressful when practised repeatedly over time. Conflicts between personal feelings and professional values can lead to alienation, emotional exhaustion and burnout (Grant and Kinman 2014). Another source of stress is fear of aggression from service users or members of the public, including hostility expressed through social media. Distress can also have organizational causes, such as a lack of management support, bullying, dealing with complaints or fear of negative media publicity (Smith 2004). It can be helpful for social workers to develop a variety of personal coping strategies (Grant and Kinman 2014) for acknowledging emotion and dealing with stress, including engagement with peer support. Garrett (2016), however, argues that seeing resilience as an individual responsibility downplays the impact of political and social factors. It is certainly true that developing individual resilience cannot address the causes of wider organizational stressors, nor the emotional impact of dealing with structural issues such as racism, homophobia and other kinds of discrimination in the workplace and in wider society (Community Care 2012; McNicoll 2013).

Exercise 4.3: How are you supported in the workplace?

- What personal coping strategies do you currently or do you intend to use in relation to your work?
- How does or might your employer and/or team support your emotional resilience?
- Based on either or both your responses, think of one or two actions that would enhance your sense of being supported at work.

Howe (2008) has argued that emotionally intelligent social workers are an organization's most important resource, and therefore need to be supported. Employers have a duty of care to their staff, and a supportive organizational culture and attention to workloads can help social workers to feel more resilient (Hussein et al. 2014). Nurturing and open team cultures make it easier for emotion to be on the agenda, both in supervision and peer discussion. In addition, organizations can engage with campaigns to address workplace stress and other social issues, such as those run by the BASW and trade unions. Your employer should also have policies to protect staff and provide support when violence or aggression occur.

A sense of professional identity

It may seem obvious that having a strong professional identity is an element of professionalism; indeed, the two may seem interchangeable. Registering as a social worker places certain expectations and obligations on you as an individual, but what we want to argue here is that this, in itself, is not enough. Just as there are diverse conceptualizations of professionalism (discussed in Chapter 2), so the term 'professional identity' is used with many different meanings and purposes. Wiles (2017) suggests that these different meanings act as resources for social workers to forge their own unique and meaningful identities as social workers, drawing on professional and personal experience and values.

A common approach is to understand professional identity in terms of professional traits, defined in regulatory and professional standards. In addition, official reports and reviews of social work convey explicit and implicit expectations about what social workers should do and what kind of people they should be. Then there is the collective sense of identity conferred by a particular social work specialism or team (Barnes et al. 2000; Moran et al. 2007; Judd and Sheffield 2010), socializing novices into professional values and ways of thinking and acting. In a multidisciplinary team, collective social work identity can also develop in contrast with other professionals (White and Featherstone 2005), and social workers may even feel that their professional identity is undermined (Karban and Smith 2010). On the other hand, in England the (PCF) implicitly conveys a shared professional identity that supersedes variations in organizational settings and roles (Scholar et al. 2014). Some practitioners may feel ambivalent about, or resistant to, social work identity, perhaps because of tensions between their personal and professional values. For example, professionalism's traditional connotations of elitism and conformity can appear at odds with the social justice values that may have called you into social work (Payne 2013).

Exercise 4.4: Your own professional identity

- To what extent is your own sense of professional identity rooted in your team or specialism?
- If you work in a multidisciplinary setting, do you feel able to have a distinct social work identity?

Harrison and Ruch (2007) make an interesting distinction between having a professional identity and – more useful in their view – being and sustaining a professional self. They suggest that an identity built solely around regulatory processes and standards is too narrow. They argue that social workers must instead develop an integrated and internalized professional identity that can sustain them through practice challenges. There is research evidence (McAllister and McKinnon 2009) that having a strong and positive sense of professional identity boosts confidence, mutual support and resilience. At the same time, social workers' collective strength may enable them to use their education, knowledge, skill and humanity to support and empower service users and communities.

Engaging actively in supervision

Reviews of social work emphasize the importance of regular, supportive and challenging professional supervision (Laming 2009; SWTF 2009). Supervision is key to professionalism because this is where social workers can engage in critical reflection, discuss ethical dilemmas and maintain a sense of professional identity. Equally, taking responsibility for one's own supervision is a hallmark of professionalism. This includes active participation by initiating items for discussion and spending time in advance preparing and thinking.

It is, however, important to distinguish between different kinds of supervision. Management supervision is primarily focused on making sure that the organization's work is progressing to a satisfactory standard. This is important and necessary, but social workers also need professional supervision that provides emotional support and the opportunity to develop (Lambley and Marrable 2013). Good supervision can, of course, combine both elements. For example, the social worker can use supervision to explore options when a decision needs to be made, and recording decisions improves accountability. Research studies suggest that it can be beneficial for social workers to have access to a supervisor from their own profession (SCIE 2013). This may be especially important when working in a multidisciplinary setting, in a team that includes a mix of roles, or in an agency or team in which you are the only qualified social worker.

Reflection point 4.3

Consider your current experience of receiving supervision, whether as a student from a lecturer or as a practitioner in the workplace:

- *Would you describe this as 'management' or 'professional' supervision, and why?*
- *Does your supervision provide the amount of support and challenge that you would like?*

If you work in an organization where professional social work supervision is not available, you may need to be proactive in seeking out additional or alternative sources of supervision, such as peer supervision with others in your team or other forms of shared learning and reflection. Co-working cases can also provide fruitful opportunities for reflection on differing perspectives and knowledge.

Application to skills
Clearly, the quality of the supervisory relationship is also key. Practitioners may feel the need to present a professional 'face' rather than admit to experiencing difficult emotional responses to their work (Ingram 2013). Supervisors need to be skilled in ensuring the practitioner feels heard and empowered, enabling anxieties and emotions to be contained (Ruch 2007; Ferguson 2011). The protected space in supervision can also make it possible to explore values and awareness of relational power dynamics, including its intersection with economic and structural inequalities.

Continuing Professional Development (CPD)

Being professional includes taking responsibility for improving your practice through appropriate professional development. This can be seen in terms of using your professional power, in the sense that you will want your interventions and decisions to be informed by relevant and up-to-date social work knowledge, research and skills. CPD can, as you know, be pursued in a variety of ways, including workplace learning, shared learning, dialogue and discussion amongst peers, attending training and development events, and following up on areas of interest through independent study or practice-based research. Your employer may offer opportunities for coaching or mentoring, and shadowing or observing can prove invaluable. Learning can also be gained through collaborative working, and through collecting and reflecting on feedback from service users and carers.

Exercise 4.5: Your opportunities for CPD

List all the ways in which you create or take up opportunities for your own CPD.

Whatever the opportunities, all forms of professional learning, new knowledge and skills take time to become consolidated and embedded into everyday practice. This is where, Higham (2013) argues, it is essential for social workers to be open to using critical reflection to further develop their professionalism, through making sense of what they have learned and applying this to their practice. They also need their employers to support, and show an active interest in, professional development. Clearly, supportive and safe professional supervision plays an important role in this respect, reinforcing new achievements and facilitating critical reflection and challenge, including analysing practice that was less successful.

CPD is embedded in regulatory and professional standards and is usually an organizational requirement. Over and above this, however, it is an opportunity to pursue your particular interests and passion for social work. This may not always be easy in times of economic recession (Higham 2013), but undertaking continued learning will enable you to maintain effective and safe practice, professional confidence and skills to help keep you motivated as an autonomous and reflective social worker.

Bringing the elements of professionalism together

This chapter began by arguing that professionalism involves integrating your knowledge, values and skills into everyday practice. The final activity will help you to explore how this works.

Exercise 4.6: Integrating professionalism in your own practice

Draw a spider diagram or another visual aid to represent the eight elements of professionalism discussed in this chapter. Now, thinking about a recent piece of your own social work practice that was complex and challenging, see if you can identify examples of how the elements of professionalism were addressed.

- Do you notice any connections and tensions between the different elements?
- Which three aspects of professionalism would you rate as the most important to you personally, and why?

Summary and conclusion

This chapter has introduced key ideas that underpin this book's approach to professional skills. First, we regard the four skills areas – self-management, communication, risk and safeguarding, and leadership – as organizing themes for thinking holistically about the skills and recognizing the interconnectness between them. Second, we suggest that the professionalism in these skill areas can be evaluated in relation to eight key elements: self-awareness about professional and personal values; the use of professional power; critical analysis; research mindedness; emotional resilience; a sense of professional identity; engaging actively in supervision; and CPD. We draw on these ideas in the remaining chapters.

Key points from this chapter

- We argued that the notion of capabilities is useful in conveying the holistic integration of professional standards relating to practical skills, personal qualities, values, knowledge and understanding.
- Professionalism involves the ability to integrate the whole of a social worker's competence into everyday social work practice.
- We view professionalism as something that each individual social worker develops and maintains across their career, building on a continual process of learning and critical reflection.

Recommended reading

McLaughlin, H. and Teater, B. (2017) Evidence-informed Practice for Social Work. London: Open University Press.

The following organizations offer useful free-of-charge resources to support a wide range of professional development:

- British Association of Social Workers (BASW): https://www.basw.co.uk/
- Social Care Institute for Excellence (SCIE): http://www.scie.org.uk/
- The Institute for Research and Innovation in Social Services (Iriss) https://www.iriss.org.uk/
- Social Care Workforce Research Unit: https://www.kcl.ac.uk/sspp/policy-institute/scwru/index.aspx
- Joseph Rowntree Foundation (JRF): https://www.jrf.org.uk/

You may also find that your employer subscribes to the following:

- Research in Practice: https://www.rip.org.uk/
- Research in Practice for Adults: https://www.ripfa.org.uk/
- Community Care Inform: http://www.communitycare.co.uk/community-care-inform-children-adults/

5 Skills for supporting people to self-manage

Chapter overview

By the end of this chapter, you will:

- Understand why in current practice social workers require most service users to change their behaviours
- Know a model of behaviour change widely applied in social work practice
- Know how to assist people to maintain change that is necessary for their safety – from the perspective of service users, this is also called self-management skills
- Understand the use of goal-setting in professional practice

Introduction

In this chapter, we explore the skills for supporting service users to transform behaviours that may be harmful to them and others, as well as for assisting them to maintain these transformations. This chapter follows on from the theoretical discussion in Chapter 3, where we described the concept of 'self-management' and developed an applicable model in social work. The premise of the ensuing discussion is that frequently social workers engage with service users who need to change or modify their behaviour as part of self-management. We therefore start by explaining the transtheoretical model (Prochaska et al. 1992), which is widely adopted in social work to explain stages of change. This is followed by an exploration of motivational interviewing (MI) skills that professionals can adopt to initiate changes in behaviour. After this, we show how social workers can enhance service users' abilities to self-manage by way of providing information. Finally, we discuss goal-setting, a skill that can enable people to set themselves targets as an incentive to meet desired objectives. We now discuss the model of change.

Theoretical context

One purpose of self-management is the involvement of service users in decision-making about their care and giving them scope to implement care plans with decreasing input from professionals. However, as we discussed in Chapter 3, this assumes that people have the *capability* and *motivation* to manage their care needs. Unfortunately, social workers frequently engage with service users who need to change their behaviour to minimize risk to themselves and others. An example is parental substance misuse, as this is associated with child neglect or harm (Brandon et al. 2014; see Bosk et al. 2017 for a critical review). In this context, consumption of alcohol and other drugs can be 'problematic behaviour' because, beyond a certain point, it can lead to harm to the adult and (potentially) the child. Any intervention with parents who misuse substances would therefore have to include measures to assist them to alter their behaviour and lifestyle. Thus, one kind of self-management involves supporting service users to change the behaviours that led to statutory intervention in the first place. This would start with an assessment of whether the service user has an insight into the harm caused by their behaviour and if they are willing and able to change. In these circumstances, being professional entails having the skill set to conduct the required assessments and plan interventions, taking into account the service user's propensity to modify their behaviour.

A model often adopted in social work is the transtheoretical model (Prochaska et al. 1992), which provides the theoretical context for this chapter. This model posits that changing problematic behaviour occurs over time. For instance, a father who misuses alcohol is unlikely to stop drinking immediately if informed that the local authority will seek a court order to place his children in foster care. Prochaska et al. (1992) suggest that transformation of such behaviour occurs over time in five *stages*, which we outline shortly.

To position the discussion firmly in practice, we will draw on a 'real' case in which one of us (G.B.) was involved as a children's safeguarding social worker. (We have given the family a fictitious name to protect their anonymity.) The case involved the Shahak family, comprising a married heterosexual couple with two children. The Shahaks were of Jewish origin. Mr Shahak served in the Israel Defense Forces when young. Due to a combination of his time in the military and physical abuse by his stepfather, Mr Shahak believed that corporal punishment was the only way of setting boundaries for his son, Isaac. Safeguarding services became involved with the family when Isaac's swimming teacher noticed that he had a large bruise on his torso. When asked, Isaac told his teacher that his father caused the bruise after kicking him repeatedly. Mr Shahak was arrested for assault and admitted to harming his son. Having outlined the illustrative practice scenario, we now discuss the five stages of change:

1. **Precontemplation:** This is the first stage in the model. At this point, 'there is no intention to change behaviour in the foreseeable future. Many individuals in this stage are unaware or underaware of their problem' (Prochaska et al. 1992: 1103). In the model, it is proposed that at this stage people will change if pressure is applied on them to do so, however they will revert to their previous behaviour once it eases. Drawing on Mr Shahak's case, although his physical abuse of Isaac caused Isaac serious injury and led to his own arrest, Mr Shahak was unwilling to change his behaviour. This is because he believed that, notwithstanding his bruises, Isaac would benefit from being set boundaries even if this was through physical abuse.
2. **Contemplation:** At this second stage, people become aware that their behaviour is problematic but they will not commit to changing. Prochaska suggests that

people can remain at this stage for a long time, perhaps for up to two years. For Mr Shahak, this stage occurred to him when he was arrested for repeatedly kicking his child. Due to concerns that he would harm Isaac again, he was bailed on condition that he did not return to the family home. Although Mr Shahak realized then that his actions had caused the police to arrest him and that it could lead to the breakdown of his family, he would not commit to changing his behaviour.

3. **Preparation:** In the transtheoretical model, this stage is accompanied by minimal yet significant alterations to problematic behaviour. While these may not be entirely successful, they nevertheless evidence the intention to change willingly. In the case of Mr Shahak, this stage was marked by him changing his aggressive nature and altering his belief in physical violence as a means of disciplining Isaac.
4. **Action:** This is the 'stage in which individuals modify their behaviour, experiences, or environment in order to overcome their problems. Action involves the most overt behavioural changes and requires considerable commitment of time and energy' (Prochaska et al. 1992: 1104). In the case of Mr Shahak, this would involve him not physically chastising Isaac.
5. **Maintenance:** This is the last stage and here people work to actively maintain the changes that they achieved in stage 4.

Prochaska argued that change does not occur linearly and sequentially, as in stages 1–5. Instead, as professionals, we should anticipate that people will 'relapse' in the sense that they are likely to revert to their previous behaviour or an earlier stage of change. As an illustration, in a hypothetical situation, when Mr Shahak reached stage 3, the preparation point, he could have attacked Isaac again. This could have led to another arrest and his reversion to stage 2, to contemplate the implications of his actions. Additionally, in deciding to change, people weigh up the advantages and disadvantages – this evaluation is called *decisional balance* (Prochaska et al. 1994). In the case of Mr Shahak, it was put to him that if he continued with his behaviour, the local authority would seek a court order to place the children in foster care to protect them. Mrs Shahak also explained to him that, without behaviour change, she would divorce him. Therefore, Mr Shahak had to balance the disadvantages of losing his children and the end of his marriage against the advantage of maintaining his beliefs about how to discipline his child.

Exercise 5.1: Reflecting on our problematic behaviours

This exercise is designed to enable you to reflect on a behaviour that you may want to change, either currently or in the future. In doing so, you should apply the concepts discussed in this chapter to your experiences.

We encourage you to do this exercise alone to aid honest self-reflection, however you can do this within a group if you trust your colleagues to maintain confidentiality.

- Identify one of your problematic behaviours. Why do you consider it to be a problem?
- Where would you position yourself on the five-stage model?
- What would motivate you to change your behaviour?

In some respects, all of us have aspects of our lives that we would like to change. However, as social workers, we are primarily concerned with those behaviours that are potentially harmful to service users or detrimental to their well-being. Examples include substance misuse, problem gambling, persistently leaving children without supervision, severe and uncontrolled anger, and unhealthful sexual relations. The transtheoretical model is useful for shaping our decisions about whether a service user is ready for change. This is because assessment of people's motivation to change can have a profound impact on the trajectory of a case. For instance, in the case of Mr Shahak, if he had informed professionals from the outset that he recognized the harm caused to his children by his form of discipline and that he would like to change, therapeutic services would have been arranged for him. This acknowledgement may also have led professionals to assess that Mr Shahak is unlikely to hit Isaac again because he realized the physical and emotional impact of his actions on his children. Having discussed the theoretical context for the chapter, we now want to explain the skills for self-management, starting with MI.

Skills for enabling people to change

In this section, we discuss some skills for facilitating change in problematic behaviour as part of self-management. We start with MI, followed by the use of written information in self-management, goal-setting and, finally, partnership working.

Motivational interviewing skills

MI is a '... *directive, client-centred counselling style for eliciting behaviour change by helping clients explore and resolve ambivalence*' (Rollnick and Miller 1995, cited in Rollnick and Allison 2004: 107). MI overlaps with self-management concepts. Recall that self-efficacy refers to confidence – if people are confident in their ability to change, then they may try to do so and they may also sustain this change (Walpole et al. 2013). Furthermore, to create a relationship conducive to change, professionals need to be empathetic and 'tune in' to the service user's needs (Stone 2016). Also, professionals need to be motivated to work with the service users, and they need good reflection skills to understand how they impact on the change process. As we showed in Chapter 3, these aforementioned attributes fall under emotional intelligence.

MI is an intervention designed to evoke change by drawing on people's own motivation. In MI, the professional combines skills – for example, asking open-ended questions and reflective listening – with the 'spirit' that they have created in their relationship with the service user. Wahab described spirit as 'the style, the way, the intention and the gestalt of the practitioner's disposition with the client'

(2005: 47). In the MI literature, 'spirit' is highlighted because theorists argue that the *relationship* between the service user and the professional is as important as the skills deployed to enact change (Miller and Rose 2009). The professional has to create a 'spirit' based on the principles of *collaboration*, *evocation* and *autonomy*.

Research note: Explaining the 'spirit' of MI

- **Collaboration:** In MI, professionals and service users are partners in the change process. This means that professionals refrain from telling service users what to do. Rather, they listen and seek to understand the service users' viewpoints. The assumption is that service users have the necessary skills to change, which professionals facilitate and harness (Hohman 2012).
- **Evocation:** The aim of professionals is to elicit the desire for change from the service user. This is not about convincing or persuading but asking open-ended questions that enable the service user to understand the need for behaviour modification, driven by themselves.
- **Autonomy:** Based on the principles of self-determination, there is a recognition that service users have the right to change or maintain their problematic behaviour(s). Thus, when operating within an MI framework, professionals eschew 'threatening' service users or coercing them to change their behaviour; the desire and reasons for change have to be articulated by the service user.

We may conceive the core aim of MI as an attempt to support people to move through the stages of change proposed by Prochaska et al. (Wahab 2005). Consequently, adopting MI in practice implies an assumption that you will conduct an assessment to determine the service user's position on the transtheoretical model, for example, whether they are at a precontemplation, contemplation or preparation stage.

Exercise 5.2: Assessing indications of motivation to change

Consider the following scenario. Suppose you are a social worker in a disabled children's team. One of the children you work with is a Moroccan boy called Ismail, who is diagnosed with autism and lives with his mother, Mary. One day you visit the family and find that Mary has a new partner, introduced to you as Alex. Later, you are contacted by the National Probation Service and informed that Alex has a conviction for violent crime and, in key working sessions with prison staff, he disclosed that he was a violent racist. In an attempt to assess the risk to Ismail, you discuss this information with Mary; she tells you that she is aware of Alex's past. She also says, 'In an ideal world, I don't want to be with a racist because I am Moroccan. But right now, his history doesn't bother me because I want and need love in my life'.

- What does this statement tell you about Mary's motivation to change?

In this scenario, we can say that Mary is at the contemplation stage because she recognizes the drawbacks of her relationship with Alex. MI techniques are designed to assist Mary to move onto a different stage of the model, where she can be motivated to prepare to end her relationship. MI is service user-led – the role of the practitioner is to assist them to explore the advantages of changing, balanced against the disadvantages of not doing so.

There are three concepts associated with the process of change in MI (Rollnick and Allison 2004). The first is *readiness*, which refers to the state of preparedness to change. The second is *ambivalence*, which refers to the state where people want to change but are unable to do so because of the benefits that they attach to their problematic behaviour. Rollnick and Allison argue that change is difficult because it involves people altering their belief systems and losing the value (however harmful) of the problematic behaviour in their lives. Thus, '[To] increase the probability of change – the client's readiness – the [social worker's] task is to encourage the client to change the balance of "weights" from one clause, "I don't want to . . ." to the other, "I want to . . ."; to shift commitment from one posture to the other' (Rollnick and Allison 2004: 108). The final concept is *resistance*: 'a general reluctance to make progress, or as opposition to the counsellor [or social worker] or what the [social worker] thinks is best, or as the client's expectations as to the posture of the agency the [social worker] represents, or even, more traditionally, as "denial"' (Rollnick and Allison 2004: 109). Here, service users oppose the imposition on them of a care plan that they have not been involved in formulating. This could take a variety of forms in social work practice, from outright hostility and lack of engagement to disguised compliance.

Most practitioners will encounter the scenarios depicted by these three concepts at some point in their career. Referring to Mary and Ismail as an example, we can say that she was not ready for change because she attached more benefits to the relationship than being single. She was, however, ambivalent because she also recognized the contradictions in a Moroccan woman having a violent racist as a partner (note, though, that she did not explore the risk to Ismail). Mary was also resistant because she did not want to countenance the possible consequences of Alex living in her home. However, as social workers, we are aware of the risk to Ismail and Mary, therefore our role will be to assist Mary to find the self-motivation to change. Change can be instigated by asking particular questions that may cause Mary to reflect on the possibility. See the examples below (adapted from University of Massachusetts Amherst 2011):

- Ask evocative questions: ask open-ended questions as they are likely to require the service user to think longer about the situation. Avoid statements that can be answered simply with 'yes/no'.
- Explore 'decisional balance': ask the service user to explore the pros and cons of change.
- Explore the negatives and positives of the problematic behaviour.
- Request elaboration on and examples of when change last occurred or instances when they have successfully changed a behaviour.

- Reflect on the past: ask about the time before the problematic behaviour occurred and explore whether things were better or different then.
- Look forward: explore with the service user what may happen if things do not change. Ask *the miracle question*: 'If you are successful in making the changes that you want, what would be different? How would you like your life to be in five years' time?'
- Explore with the service user the extreme scenario of maintaining the status quo: 'What are the worst things that might happen if you do not make this change?' Alternatively, 'What is the best thing that might happen if you make this change?'
- Explore the service user's goals and values: this would include what they want in life and examining how their problematic behaviour could impede their attainment of their goals.
- Explore the importance of the problematic behaviour with the service user: 'Perhaps this is so important to you that you will not give it up irrespective of the cost'.

You can see from the preceding discussion that MI draws on good communication skills and issues of power, discussed later in Chapter 6. The questions invite the service user to talk and reflect on their situation; the corollary is that the professional listens to them. Rollnick et al. (2010) suggest that one way to demonstrate to service users that we have listened is to repeatedly summarize what we've heard. There is also the need to demonstrate empathy for their conditions and refraining from judging them.

Summary

- MI skills are useful in self-management because, by drawing on these, professionals can enable service users to consider the need to modify their behaviour.
- Professionals ask evocative questions and create a positive 'spirit' of listening, understanding, empathy and empowerment to provide a safe space for service users to reflect on their difficult behaviour.
- There is a growing evidence base that MI can be useful in self-directed change in substance misuse and, increasingly, MI is being adopted in social work (Hohman 2012).
- In the model of self-management discussed in Chapter 3, MI is useful at the point where service users need to transform their behaviours. For instance, a service user diagnosed with schizophrenia who regularly smokes cannabis, which is known to pose further risks to their mental health.
- Instead of changing their harmful behaviours, sometimes service users need information to manage their own care.

Using written information in self-management

Another way to achieve self-management is to provide information to service users to reduce the need for professional interventions in their lives. The goal here is to enable service users to increase their understanding of their situation and provide signposts to viable solutions for their difficulties.

Exercise 5.3: Kinds of information in social work

You can do this exercise on your own or as part of a group of four colleagues or friends.

- Write down the formal and informal sources of information in social work.
- *How will you determine whether to provide this to service users?*
- *How can you assist a service user to incorporate them in their own self-management?*

There are different kinds of information in social work. There are *formal* sources such as government documents, internal organization policies and records, journals, and official papers from fellow professionals. These all tend to be written. However, there are also *informal* sources such as information from other service users, telephone conversations with professionals, leaflets and the internet.

Written information can be in a variety of formats, including leaflets about services provided by charities and voluntary organizations in a locality, website addresses, telephone helplines, text messages, and any other sources of electronic information (de Silva 2011). To be useful in self-management, these can be personalized and targeted to service users' needs.

For example, in the case of service users with learning difficulties, the information would have to be accessible, including short sentences and visual images (see Chapter 6 for a discussion of communication skills). Sometimes it may be helpful to explain in written form *why* and *how* service users' conduct has led to statutory intervention. In safeguarding work, service users should be given copies of the assessment, case records and the care plans, which together explain the concerns about their care of their child(ren) and/or themselves. In order for this kind of self-management to be successful, service users ought to have the mental capacity to understand information and the associated risk of their actions (DCA 2005, 2007). They also need to have literacy skills to read the information provided. Finally, there is an implicit assumption in this model that service users are capable of, and motivated to, self-manage. The next section is about goal-setting for service users, which is based on the assumption discussed latterly.

Goal-setting skills

A goal is an outcome that we desire to achieve and for which we plan, commit time and devote resources to attain. Goals are linked to self-efficacy (Eccles and Wigfield 2002) because as we accomplish them we increase our self-confidence in our ability to meet other goals. Some themes in this section will be familiar to you because we discussed them under the Research note in Chapter 3 – a study by Carpenter et al. (2015) on self-efficacy. In that section, we explained that self-efficacy theory suggests that as we successfully complete a task, we become more confident because our belief in our capabilities also grows. In addition to the underpinning ideas explored here, researchers have outlined the principles of goal-setting, as detailed in Table 5.1.

In addition to these principles, we can think of goals as divided into short- and long-term goals. Let us use the example of an adult who wants to stop misusing substances to illustrate this point further.

Exercise 5.4: Exploring short- and long-term goals

Suppose that, as a new employee in a local authority substance misuse team, you have been allocated to work with Mr Abrahams, who has been assessed as motivated to change. He would like to stop misusing substances.

- Write a table of the short- and long-term goals that Mr Abrahams has to achieve to realize his aims.

In this example, the long-term goal may be obvious, however the short-term ones may be less so. Taking the work of Bandura cited in Table 5.1 as a guide, Mr Abrahams may have to focus on short-term and relatively small achievable steps, such as reducing the quantity of drugs taken daily, engaging in new leisure activities and reducing his contact with his peers who also abuse substances. These are incremental steps that Mr Abrahams can take. However, together these are significant, as they will increase Mr Abrahams' self-efficacy and sustain his motivation to stop abusing substances. This may, nevertheless, present a tension for professionals because if there are identified risks with his lifestyle, we may want him to stop *immediately*. On the other hand, as we have explained in the commentary to point 3 in Table 5.1, telling Mr Abrahams to quit his habit suddenly would appear too difficult to him and thus demotivate him. One way to maintain Mr Abrahams' desire to change is to set goals *with* him – this is a model of partnership working.

Partnership working skills

This is a model that proposes that professionals and service users work as equal experts to set goals and enable the latter to manage their care. For this to be

Table 5.1 Selected principles of goal-setting

Principle	Commentary
1. Goals that are specific, immediate and difficult promote self-efficacy (Bandura 1994 and Schunk 1990 cited in Eccles and Wigfield 2002)	If people are pushed a little outside their comfort zone and are set short-term and specific goals, they become more confident when they attain them.
2. Goals that are specific are more likely to lead to self-evaluation than those that are general (Schunk 1990)	If we want people to reflect on their abilities, then set them specific goals. For example: 'On Tuesday, please get your son Alex to school at 8:15 am' is better than 'Please ensure that Alex gets to school on time'. This is because, unlike the second, the first goal includes an identified day and time, making it easier to understand and follow.
3. There is a relationship between the difficulty of a task and the effort committed (Locke and Latham 2002)	Moderately difficult tasks elicit the highest commitment from people; however, when we are set easy or very difficult tasks, we may be demotivated. This is because we may feel that the task does not require much effort or, alternatively, it is unachievable. An example of a difficult goal that could easily demotivate a service user is telling someone who consumes two bottles of wine daily to stop drinking immediately otherwise the local authority will initiate proceedings to place their child in foster care.
4. Specific and difficult goals lead to higher performance than simply saying 'do your best' (Locke and Latham 2002)	It is better to set definitive expectations for ourselves or service users than simply saying 'improve' or 'do better'.
5. If people set their own goals and meet them, they are likely to modify other behaviour (DeWalt et al. 2009).	This relates to the discussion of MI: change is more likely to be sustained if people find self-motivation to do so.

effective, the service user takes the lead in identifying what they believe to be their problematic behaviours and conduct. The professional's role is to assist the service user to identify solutions. It has been shown that where service users believe that professionals listen to them, give them attention, empathize with them and encourage their participation in establishing care plans, self-management is likely to be successful (Corben and Rosen 2005). In Table 5.2, we explain how this model operates in practice.

There are some important features of this table, worthy of further exposition. You can see that in this model, the service user's motivation is a prerequisite for success. Thus, there is an implicit assumption of the service user's desire to participate and find solutions to their difficulties. A second point, which follows on from this, is that the social worker will conduct an assessment of the service

Table 5.2 Working with a partnership model in self-management

Issue	How this is addressed in a partnership model
What is the relationship between the service user and social worker?	Both are experts (McLaughlin 2009). The social worker understands the legal issues and how to harness statutory services to enable the service user to address the 'problems' that they have identified. The service user is an expert on their life.
Who is responsible for a successful outcome?	Both social worker and service user. However, the former may be legally accountable for the safety of the latter – for instance, 'vulnerable service users'.
What is the goal?	The service user identifies goals, which the social worker assists them to attain by providing information to enable them to make informed choices. Together, the social worker and service user develop strategies for meeting the goals.
How is behaviour changed?	The service user has self-motivation to change.
How are problems identified?	By the service user. This could result from provision of information from the social worker or the service user can identify their problems.
How are problems solved?	Social worker and service user jointly develop problem-solving skills.

Source: Adapted from Bodenheimer et al. (2002).

user's motivation to change, for example, drawing on Prochaska et al. (1992). A third point about this model is that the social worker has to know their statutory duties. Recall that in Chapter 1 we explained that the professional title 'social worker' entails discharging statutory duties. This means that in some instances, the law and statutory guidance explain what social workers *should* do in certain situations. For example, *Working Together to Safeguard Children* (DfE 2015) outlines the duties of local authorities towards children who are at risk. This means that, irrespective of the service user's motivation to change, as a social worker you have to follow those procedures, thereby reducing the scope for self-management using this model.

We now provide two practice scenarios, which are designed to expand your learning and encourage you to reflect further on the partnership model of self-management.

Exercise 5.5: Partnership working – understanding the interface with statutory duties

Suppose you are the social worker on duty in an older people's team. You are allocated two cases: one about Mrs Samuels and the other about Mr Solomos, which came to the attention of the service a week ago. The current information about both service users is as follows.

Mrs Samuels
Mrs Samuels is a retired police officer who lives alone in a ground floor flat and uses a wheelchair. Mrs Samuels' neighbour, Mrs Aldo, contacted the older people's team because of concerns that she is neglecting herself. Mrs Aldo also reported that Mrs Samuels ate unhealthful food, lived in an untidy house and abused alcohol.

Mr Solomos
Mr Solomos has lived in his home for 20 years. He is known to services as a 'vulnerable adult' who allows strangers to come to his house to drink alcohol. It is explained in the referral that Mr Solomos once told a professional that the reason why he invited people to his house was because he was 'lonely'. The current referral noted increased concerns about Mr Solomos because of reports that his house is being used as the base for selling illegal drugs.

Drawing on the discussion to date, consider the following:

- What are the presenting issues for both Mrs Samuels and Mr Solomos?
- What questions would you ask as part of your assessment to determine whether a partnership model of self-management is applicable?
- Consider the skills that you can draw upon in this case.

Reflection point 5.1

The referrals for Mrs Samuels and Mr Solomos are complex yet not unfamiliar examples of complicated issues that social workers encounter. Readers will identify the presenting issues as: self-neglect and substance misuse (Mrs Samuels) and risk of physical harm and arrest (Mr Solomos). To practise within the partnership model of self-management, there is a need to assess whether each service user is motivated to change by asking such questions as:

- *What part of their actions do they consider problematic, and why?*
- *How much do they want to change their behaviour? (This question is aimed at ascertaining the stage they are at on the Prochaska et al. [1992] model.)*
- *Have Mrs Samuels and Mr Solomos attempted to change in the past?*
- *Will the service users modify their actions if they're provided with information about different options – for instance, information about local befriending volunteers?*

Application to skills
The skills required in the case that readers may identify include communication, empathy, understanding of the law and safeguarding procedures, research skills (to understand the complex issues) and analysis.

A related matter that the referrals show is that Mrs Samuels and Mr Solomos are experiencing self-neglect because of their inability or unwillingness to consider their safety in their decision-making. In the case of Mr Solomos, this is compounded by risk of physical harm and arrest because of the presence of hard drugs in his house. In England, there are procedures for social workers to follow where adult service users are at risk (DoH 2016). Professionals must assess the risk to service users within a multi-professional framework and create a plan to protect the service user. In making these plans, there is scope to empower service users and incorporate their motivation and capabilities to implement safeguarding plans (Romeo 2015). However, professionals must conduct a safeguarding assessment first, irrespective of the service user's motivation to change or work with professionals to mitigate the situation. These circumstances can be taken into account when establishing the safeguarding plans.

Summary and conclusion

This chapter has explored the professional skills for assisting service users to oversee their care and manage their needs to reduce statutory intervention. The chapter started with a discussion of a model of change comprised of five stages. It was important to discuss this model because there are occasions when people have to change their lifestyles to reduce risks to themselves and/or others. This is self-management because the transformation will occur through their own actions. Another technique discussed in this section is MI, which is currently considered to be an important skill in social work. MI complements the earlier exploration of stages of change because it is a means of enabling people to contemplate the need for behaviour modification. After the discussion of MI, we discussed the use of written information in self-management, goal-setting and partnership working. These last skills may be useful when professionals assess that people are ready to modify their lifestyles or that they don't need to change any problematic behaviours. A related skill that professionals need to develop to enable change in service users is communication, which we discuss next.

Key points from this chapter

- The principles of self-management can be drawn upon to assist service users to change problematic behaviours or oversee their care plans with minimal professional intervention.
- The skills for doing this include MI, where professionals assist service users to recognize the need for change and commit to doing so. Theoretically and

ethically, change cannot be imposed on people, rather they have to become aware of the need for change.

- The transtheoretical model postulates that 'relapse' is intrinsic to processes of behaviour change.
- Professionals can draw on goal-setting skills to assist service users to manage their care. In so doing, there are principles that engender successful attainment of goals. These include the need for specific, attainable but challenging goals.

Recommended reading

Oliver, B. and Pitt B. (2013) *Engaging Communities and Service Users: Context, Themes and Methods*. Basingstoke: Palgrave Macmillan.

6 Communication skills

Chapter overview

By the end of this chapter, you will:

- Understand the role of communication skills in professionalism
- Know how professional communication can take account of unequal power
- Be able to use social work values to review a range of communication situations
- Know how to apply critical reflection and empathy in challenging contexts

Introduction

As their career progresses, social workers find themselves dealing with increasingly high-risk and complex situations in which interactions may be characterized by intense emotions, tensions, conflicts and hostility. However successful you are as a communicator, there is a case for standing back from habitual patterns to analyse your skills afresh. Gast and Bailey (2014) argue in favour of maintaining what they refer to as 'conscious competence': the stage just before competence becomes second nature. This chapter does not seek to 'teach' communication skills, but rather to stimulate reflection on how your practice thereof can be enhanced by professionalism. Selected communication topics and practice examples will be discussed with a view to providing resources to help you gain new insights into your own communication experiences. Effective communication does not require you to be expert in every type of situation; but understanding how service users are disadvantaged by poor communication motivates you to continue developing your repertoire of skills and confidence. Further learning resources are listed at the end of this chapter.

Exercise 6.1: Reflection on a recent encounter

Take a few minutes to reflect on a recent social work situation where communication was difficult. Alternatively, recall a similar challenge in your working or personal life.

Write two or three bullet points identifying the factors that challenged you – for example, those relating to the context or your own feelings. You may wish to compare your skills with those outlined in professional standards, such as the Knowledge and Skills Statements, and draw up an inventory of which skills you feel confident about and which ones you want to develop further.

The importance of a positive professional relationship, through which social workers can create change with service users, has regained interest in recent years (Trevithick 2003; Ruch et al. 2010). Whether a social work relationship is relatively brief or develops over a longer period, good communication skills are needed to build it. Effective communication is not a stand-alone skill but goes hand in hand with the ability to draw on a theoretical understanding of human behaviour and a critically reflective awareness of one's own self and values.

We begin by considering one of the elements of professionalism introduced in Chapter 4: the appropriate and ethical use of professional power in relation to language and communication. You are then invited to revisit the core conditions of good communication in the light of professional values. Keeping issues of values and power in mind, we then consider how these core elements of communication can be maintained in a select range of complex situations. Throughout the chapter, you will draw on critical analysis and identify areas for your CPD.

Communication and the use of professional power

Much social work communication takes place in the context of unequal power relations and in situations characterized by distress, despair or fear. As discussed in Chapter 4, social workers hold a lot of organizational power in relation to service users, even when they perceive their actual autonomy to be limited. Power is closely bound up with language. The way that ideas and actions are communicated can have a material effect on how people are viewed and treated in social work contexts.

The word 'language' has different connotations, but in the context of the UK's wide cultural diversity it commonly refers to modes of speech associated with a specific country or community. People who speak minority languages can find themselves excluded from key areas of social activity and be discouraged from using their first language in formal interactions such as medical appointments. Survey data indicates that speakers of regional accents and dialects, such as Cockney or those found in Liverpool and the West Midlands, may, similarly, face prejudice in education and employment (Dathan 2013).

Communication can also be obstructed by misunderstandings about unwritten cultural rules regarding non-verbal communication, greetings, gestures and touch.

Language is part of our identity, and in stressful or life-changing situations, service users may need to express themselves in their first language. Indeed, the Care Act 2014 (section 9[5], along with the statutory guidance) makes it a requirement of social workers that they consider a person's communication needs when carrying out an assessment, in some circumstances with the assistance of an independent advocate or specialist interpreter. Working with interpreters requires sensitivity because it can be difficult to achieve rapport and to gauge how far complex or emotionally-charged meanings are being translated. Some service users are reluctant to have an interpreter from their own community, owing to issues of stigma, confidentiality or even fear.

The Equality Act 2010 requires 'reasonable adjustments' – including the use of interpreters or signing – to be made when providing services for deaf or deaf–blind people. Taking this a step further, the British Deaf Association (2018) argues that deaf people are a linguistic minority who have the *right* to communicate in either signing or speech. Scotland became the first part of the UK to recognize this right in passing the British Sign Language (Scotland) Act 2015.

The ability to utilize the nuances of meaning is another source of language power. Social workers are often very adept at using words skilfully to persuade or to exercise authority. One example from solution-focused and brief therapy approaches is their very precise and particular use of language to promote *change*. The practitioner/therapist listens carefully and respectfully to the service user's description of the problem, but then focuses their own talk around exploring solutions. Typical questions draw out the person's view of what life would be like if the problem was resolved, moving on to elicit instances of where the desired behaviour, however infrequent and partial, is already happening (or has happened in the past). This kind of talk conveys the expectation that service users have the capacity to make positive changes. A mental health practitioner, for example, would acknowledge a person's deep distress but also affirm the positive step they had taken to seek help (Kondrat 2014).

Exercise 6.2: Persuasive language

Think about a recent occasion when you have used language to persuade a service user, colleague or another person who did not share your view. How effective were you? And how should we gauge the effectiveness of persuasive language?

You might have recalled how skilfully you were able to reframe a colleague's despondent account of an apparently fruitless meeting with a withdrawn teenager, for instance, supporting your colleague to acknowledge small gains that can be built on. Less positively, perhaps you experienced relief at having negotiated a reduced care package with a dissatisfied carer. Each of these examples illustrates the powerful effects of using carefully chosen language skills to control or mediate another person's response.

We can also use the term 'language' to refer to shared knowledge and values. In this sense, speaking the same language creates a sense of empowerment and identity in professional teams (White and Featherstone 2005); however, professional terminology – as well as what might be called 'professional shorthand' – can easily tip over into pathologizing and exclusionary language if used without awareness. How might it feel, for example, to hear your family described as 'dysfunctional' or 'chaotic', and how would you explain labels such as 'frequent flyer' or 'bed blocker' (Duffy 2017) to a loved one? Even the oft-heard 'Mum' or 'Dad' used instead of a parent's name can appear dismissive. In certain circumstances, social workers need to assist service users to interpret legal or medical terms that can arouse anxiety or confusion.

Exercise 6.3: Everyday practice language

Consider some of the terms that you have heard routinely used in your day-to-day practice, in a care agency with which you are familiar or in cases you have read about.

- To what extent might this language have an empowering or restrictive impact on the way that service users are perceived and the quality of services they are offered?

Once social workers become aware of the negative effects of disempowering language, they can look for ways to use professional power to communicate in a more positive and enabling way.

Professional values as a foundation for good communication

Our interactions do not only communicate information, they also say something about our professional relationships. Carl Rogers' (1961) concept of the working alliance between a service user and practitioner, which we might call 'partnership', recognizes the dynamic and interactive nature of social work intervention, regardless of its duration, and highlights each contact as an opportunity to create and sustain a productive relationship. Within this partnership, social work values guide the tone of communication and improve service users' experiences of the intervention, even when there is conflict (Ferguson 2011). Rogers' core conditions for person-centred counselling – unconditional positive regard, congruence (or genuineness) and empathic understanding – are closely aligned with social work values.

Unconditional positive regard involves valuing the individual, being non-judgemental, showing respect, and communicating compassion for each person's strengths, flaws and potential. *Congruence* involves being genuine and 'real' in one's dealings with the other person – for example, if you feel moved by a person's story, you would show this rather than simply presenting a 'professional façade'. *Empathic understanding* – often defined as entering another person's world without losing sight of one's own (Kondrat 2014) – involves active listening and demonstrating your understanding of the service user's perspective. Social workers can find this challenging when experiencing negative emotions in response to a service user's circumstances or behaviour. In this event, professionalism includes acknowledging one's own emotional reaction, and preferably seeking professional supervision.

Exercise 6.4: A difficult first conversation

The following communication example is fictional, modelled on real situations reported in research studies (Forrester and Harwin 2006; Holland et al. 2014;

Broadhurst et al. 2015). It shows a difficult first encounter in which unwelcome news must be shared. In particular, a mother's (who we will name Sarah) baby daughter has been looked after by the local authority since birth, and care proceedings are currently taking place following a pre-birth assessment. Tracey, a social worker, has been assigned to the case at this point, and today's home visit is her first meeting with Sarah.

- Read the conversation and try to identify Rogers' (1961) core conditions.
- Pay attention to the way language is used. Thinking about the use of professional power and values, suggest feedback for Tracey about the strengths and shortcomings in her communication and relationship-building skills.

Tracey: Hi Sarah, I'm Tracey Brown from the Children's Team. Sorry I'm late – so much traffic!

[This is followed by Tracey introducing herself and then there is some 'small talk' about the weather while they settle themselves. Tracey then explains that she has come to start an assessment of Sarah's parenting ability.]

Tracey: So, Sarah, I've been looking at the previous notes and it's fantastic to see all the changes you've made to your life. You're looking great, and the flat too. But looking at this letter from your GP, I need to be honest with you, I'm quite worried that you're still using methadone.

Sarah: Um, what do you mean? I'm off drugs now, aren't I?

Tracey: Well, you're off heroin. The thing is that, as I was explaining to you just now, I have to assess you and write a report for the court – and I'm going to need to assure the court that you are able to live drug-free for a sustained period before they could consider you having your daughter back. At present, I wouldn't be able to say that.

Sarah: [long pause, then speaks quietly] That's not fair. I know there's other people on methadone who've got their kids living with them.

Tracey: Well, I have to focus on your own situation and the risks for your daughter. And, unfortunately, there are some other factors here – like I'm aware that you've already had two other babies taken into care because of your drug use. So, that makes the risk bigger and I have to take that into account.

Sarah: But look at all the changes I've made. Surely that counts for something?

Tracey: Of course it does, Sarah. I'm not meaning to take that away from you – you've done brilliantly in that way. But I work with a lot of families in care proceedings and I just have to be totally honest with you. In addition to all the big changes you've already made, the court is going to want to see complete detox.

Sarah: But how come I never heard this before today? If I'd known, maybe . . .

Tracey: Yeah, this is something the other social worker should have explained to you. But there is still time to make the changes, Sarah. Look at what you've achieved already.

Sarah: [crying] You say that but . . . I won't ever get her back, will I? Everything I've done is just a waste of time. I've messed it up again. I won't get her back. [She sobs for some time.] I can't talk about this any more, Tracey. Please just go away.

Tracey: [long silence] Tell me . . . what are you thinking right now? Are you scared you wouldn't manage that next step? What is it that concerns you the most?

(Adapted from 'Protecting Our Children', Episode 3 (2012). [TV programme] BBC Bristol).

Reflection point 6.1

We cannot tell very much about Tracey's body language and other non-verbal communication, which limits our evaluation. Nevertheless, there is a sense that Tracey tries to build a respectful rapport with Sarah. She is clear and honest about the power she holds, while showing empathy in recognizing and exploring Sarah's fears about what may happen.

Tracey tries to convey a non-judgemental stance in affirming (and reaffirming) the effort and progress that Sarah has made. Balancing 'genuineness' with clarity about one's professional role can be challenging in social work, but in this extract Tracey seems to manage this well. On the other hand, perhaps you experienced mixed feelings when she said that the other social worker should have explained things more clearly.

- *What feedback would you offer Tracey about this point?*

There is some debate about how easily Rogers' core conditions can be applied when social workers need to be directive with service users due to time or organizational constraints, or when immediate action needs to be taken to protect a child or adult (Miller 2005; Kondrat 2014). On the other hand, you can probably recognize the influence of Rogers' core conditions in most social work approaches such as solution-focused, strengths-based, person-centred, crisis intervention or MI methods.

Exercise 6.5: Reflection on practice

Think about a recent social work conversation that you had with a service user, or with someone else who needed help from you.

- To what extent do you feel you showed genuineness, unconditional positive regard and empathy? What factors made this difficult?

Empathy is a quality that social workers are usually assumed to possess or acquire. However, research suggests that experienced social workers do not always utilize their empathy skills. Analysing 24 recordings of simulated child protection scenarios, Forrester et al. (2008) found that social workers were skilled at expressing their concerns clearly. On the other hand, they generally demonstrated low levels of empathy – tending to ask closed questions and rarely identifying strengths or positive factors. While the research could not necessarily replicate what happens in actual social work encounters, the response of the simulated service users was very interesting. However skilled the social worker was in identifying child protection concerns, the quality that overcame service users' resistance and encouraged them to share information was *empathy*. Parallels are reported in studies of adult safeguarding (Lawson et al. 2014a), in which taking a person-centred – rather than procedurally-led – approach enabled people to have more honest conversations about concerns and solutions.

So far, then, we have considered that professionalism in social work communication involves the self-aware use of professional power and values. Next, we examine a further example of how professionalism can enhance communication when verbal skills are limited.

Enhancing communication when verbal skills are limited

Some communication situations are challenging – for both the practitioner and service user – due to a reliance on non-verbal skills. Examples include interactions with adults who have advanced dementia or aphasia following a stroke, and with adults and children where cognitive or other conditions prevent or limit verbal communication. A high degree of empathy is required when working with people whose communication is impaired, challenging social workers to uphold their professionalism in terms of values, rights and power.

According to Neil Thompson (2011), communication difficulties should be understood in the light of the social model of disability. The social model holds that a medical condition or impairment is not a restriction in itself but that it is society, through discriminatory attitudes, actions and omissions, that disables people. So, a person's communication difficulty is no justification for denying them the opportunity for self-expression and social interaction. Social workers may need to use their power to challenge organizational obstacles that include: professional jargon; conventions about organizing and chairing meetings; the lack of technology such as hearing loops; or the availability of an interpreter. At the individual level, when working with people who have communication impairments, social workers can use their professional skills to convey empathy, value and respect by working with patience and sensitivity. This is important when conducting an assessment or a review with service users who have communication or cognitive difficulties, including dementia. As an example, how might you avoid the pitfalls illustrated in the following unsuccessful conversation?

Exercise 6.6: An example of unsuccessful communication in a care home

Take a few moments to reflect on this anonymized conversation overheard by one author when visiting a relative in a residential care home. Suggest what would have enabled the resident with dementia (let's call her Eileen) to communicate effectively with the care worker.

Care worker: How are you today, Eileen?

Eileen: Very well, thank you, nurse.

Care worker: Have you been out in the mini-bus today, Eileen?

Eileen: Oh yes.

Care worker: That's grand. Where did you go?

Eileen: I went – I went [pause] – we went – I don't remember . . .

Care worker: Did you go to the garden party? And did you see your sister there?

Eileen: Sister? Did I see . . . did I? Oh dear . . . I think she . . .

Care worker: [interrupting] No, she couldn't go, could she? What do you think of this weather, Eileen? Is it hot enough for you? Now tell me, Eileen, where was it you used to live before you came here?

Eileen: I lived . . . the hotel. Did I? Or was that . . . um . . . oh dear, oh dear.

Care worker: So, you used to work in a hotel, did you?

Eileen: No. Not . . . oh dear . . . It was.

Care worker: [interrupting] I heard you were a cook, Eileen.

Eileen: I cooked?

Care worker: Did you?

Eileen: I think it was my own hotel. Was it? Oh dear, dear, dear.

Eileen, who once ran her own hotel and employed several staff, was left upset and confused by this unsuccessful exchange. What this illustrates is that the most important – and yet very simple – skill is allowing people sufficient time to process what has been said and formulate a response, and avoid interrupting even if you think you know what the person is trying to say.

Australian research by Baker et al. (2015) analysed social interactions in a care home to examine the skills required for inclusive conversations with people with dementia. They found that it was easier for people with dementia to participate in conversations when the staff member picked up and provided clues, thus minimizing frustrating misunderstandings. This requires careful listening and paying particular attention to your own and the other person's body language. Empathy and positive regard are also important: reflecting back the person's meaning, even in a seemingly formulaic conversational exchange, acknowledges and respects their contribution and establishes rapport. It may be helpful to supplement speaking with appropriate facial expressions and, in some situations, carefully judged use of touch such as reassuring pats on the arm.

One form of non-verbal expression that can be misunderstood is 'challenging' behaviour, which may be an individual's way of controlling their environment and communicating their needs and wishes. Cognitive behavioural theories suggest that a pattern of challenging behaviour needs to be addressed in a positive and constructive way that supports the person to communicate (LaVigna and Donnellan 1986; Paley 2013).

Supporting communication with pictures, symbols and other visual aids

Where verbal skills are limited, both children and adults may benefit from the support of visual aids. Care UK (2015) provides a wealth of practical suggestions for carers to enhance communication with people living with dementia. For example, holding up a choice of clothing encourages a decision about what someone would like to wear. If the person is going on a trip, carers could set out their outdoor clothes and show them a photograph of the place or people they will be visiting. A photograph album can help to preserve the person's identity and provide clues to significant events or people. Creating reminiscence books or boxes (containing items associated with the person's previous hobbies, community or workplace) can prompt discussion about preferences and emotions. In many cases, sensory adaptations of these methods could be made for people who have sight loss. Life story work, already well-established for looked-after children and young people, can also benefit people who have dementia (R. Thompson 2011). The collaborative process encourages better communication and person-centred care, and develops greater understanding of the person's needs and wishes. Dementia UK (2017) provides a template for creating life story books and suggests making digital copies to guard against loss or damage.

Other communication approaches have been specifically developed for people with learning disabilities who cannot use verbal language. Picture cards, for example, enable a person to communicate their preferences or wishes in response to specific themes. Another use of pictures is to produce a visual record of reviews and meetings for people with learning disabilities, often used within the person-centred planning approach. Typically, tools such as MAPs and PATH (HSA n.d.)

use simple but expressive line drawings to create a timeline indicating key events and relationships, and the person's hopes and aspirations for the future.

The Makaton system of signs and symbols (Figure 6.1), used alongside speech, facial expression, eye contact and body language, is another means for children and adults with learning disabilities to communicate when they have unclear or no speech. It can be used at whatever level suits the individual and their needs, whether to communicate emotions and preferences or to refer to specific objects, activities or places.

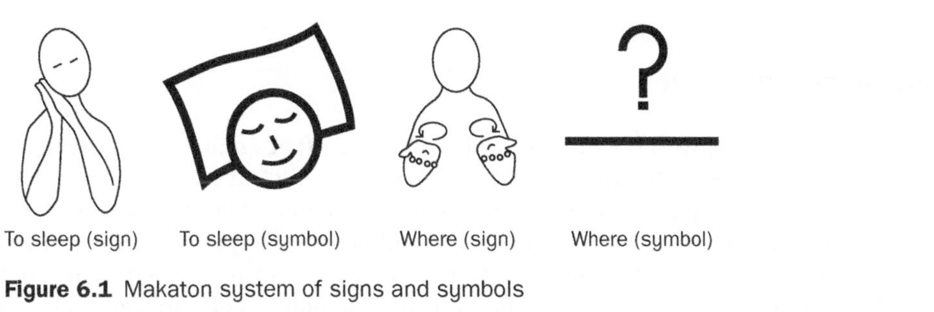

Figure 6.1 Makaton system of signs and symbols
Source: The Makaton Charity (n.d.).

Exercise 6.7: Reflection on your communication where verbal skills were limited

If you have experienced a situation where communication with a child or adult was limited by speech difficulties, reflect on how this may have impacted on their rights and choices.

- What skills and approaches did you use to overcome this (or, with hindsight, what skills would you have liked to be more competent in)?
- How do these skills relate to professionalism?

When communicating through language is neither possible nor sufficient, assessment can involve spending time with a child or adult, observing how they relate to their environment, their body language and other non-verbal clues that can indicate distress or fear. For babies and infants, Ferguson (2011) recommends picking them up in a friendly, natural way in the presence of their parent or another adult (and, of course, observing other appropriate boundaries). In some situations, you may judge that a child or adult – because of complex communication needs – would benefit from an independent advocate to help them explore options and communicate their views. At other times, the potential conflict between a service user's wishes and the agency's broader agenda means that an independent advocate may support the person to challenge a decision about their care.

UK legislation provides for independent advocacy, with some nation-specific variations. In England, for example, local authorities have a legal duty to provide and promote access to advocacy under the Mental Health Act 1983, the Mental Capacity Act 2005 and the Care Act 2014. Conversely, it can be difficult to access advocacy services where there is no statutory obligation.

While it is important to be aware of different communication methods, social workers must equally recognize that any form of communication still needs to take place within a respectful professional relationship, and be suited to the individual and the situation. This can require creativity based on critical engagement with the particular situation, informed by professional knowledge, skills and values.

Direct work with children

Working directly with children, through play and other creative approaches, can help social workers to gain understanding of the child's world and may provide essential information in safeguarding work or when a child needs to be accommodated. Using toys, dolls, hats, masks, photographs, pictures (for example, depicting faces with different emotions), drawing and play dough can enable children to express their needs, emotions and thoughts (Lefevre 2008). Life-path diagrams, timelines, genograms and ecomaps can all be adapted with the use of colours, drawings or pictures to represent events, relationships and feelings. Life story books can be created if the work extends over a number of sessions. Older children and young people may enjoy creative writing activities, or a mixture of writing and drawing. For example, they can be invited to add their own words to pictures – thought bubbles, jigsaw pieces, signposts – representing likes, dislikes, fears and aspirations. There are many sources of guidance for conducting these activities, some of which are listed at the end of this chapter.

A number of custom-designed resources are also available, such as the picture assessment tools designed for use with children and young people in safeguarding situations (Turnell and Murphy 2017). These enable a child's perspective to be expressed, and can also provide children with an understanding of what has happened to them and their family. A well-known tool is the 'Three Houses' (Weld 2008), which Figure 6.2 depicts in the adapted form used within the Signs of Safety child protection model (Turnell and Murphy 2017). A tool of this kind could be adapted for older children and young people, and used to explore different contexts such as the school environment.

'Three Houses' was first developed in New Zealand, by Nikki Weld, as a strengths-based and solution-focused tool for social workers to use in everyday work with families. The simple visual representation provides a framework to help children identify strengths, express worries, and articulate their hopes and dreams for the future. Weld emphasizes that the tool should support, rather than replace, a conversation underpinned by the professional relationship and a spirit of partnership (Weld 2017, personal communication, 10 October). The social worker presents the three blank houses to the child (a separate page for each one works well), or the child draws their own. Most practitioners commence with the 'House of Good Things', asking the child to draw and describe the positive things they enjoy there. Meanwhile, the 'House of Worries' explores things that worry or upset the child and

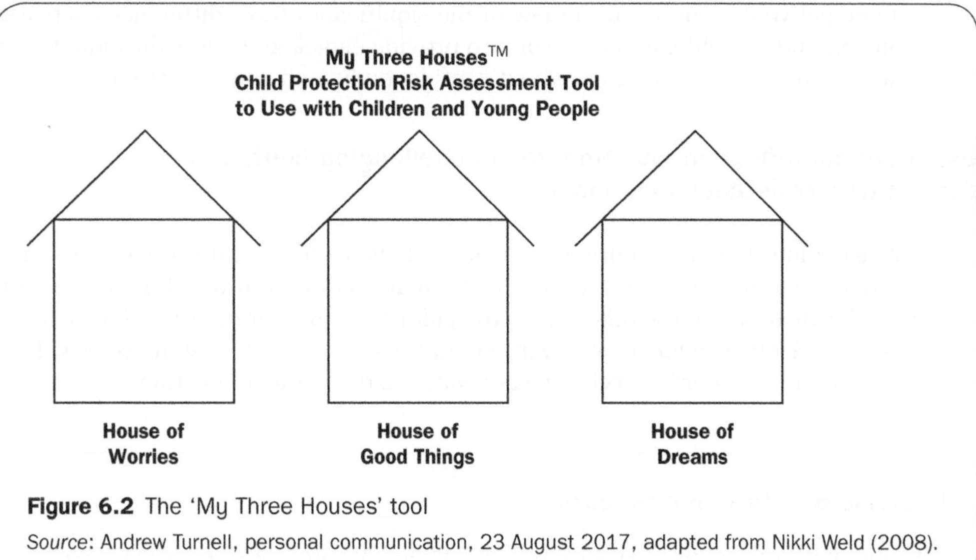

Figure 6.2 The 'My Three Houses' tool

Source: Andrew Turnell, personal communication, 23 August 2017, adapted from Nikki Weld (2008).

the 'House of Dreams' seeks to elicit the child's vision of how they would like things to be, including the people and behaviours that would facilitate this. With the child's permission, the drawings can be shared and discussed with their parents/carers.

Exercise 6.8: Reflection on communication with a child

Imagine that, as a social worker, you need to determine how a child or young person feels about returning to their parents after living with a foster family. Alternatively, reflect on a real situation where you have worked with a child or young person.

- What skills would you use to find out about the child's perspective?
- Make a note of how you might enhance your skills by using or adapting play and other non-verbal tools.
- What practical and ethical issues would you need to consider?

Gain new ideas from the resource section of this chapter.

Careful planning, sensitivity, experience and confidence are needed to introduce and use these powerful techniques in a relaxed and participatory way, and the time and pace need to be carefully managed to allow for 'winding down' at the end of the session. Consent from children and their parents is essential. Some techniques are best approached only when the social worker has access to specialist training and supervision. Whichever methods are used, it is important to communicate a genuine interest in the child and a willingness to understand their perspective. Successful communication with children also requires an understanding of their emotional and cognitive development. In view of the significant power differences between yourself and the child, it is important to provide choice and allow the child to opt out of activities and to be clear about confidentiality and any limits to this.

Using critical reflection and empathy in challenging contexts: dealing with resistance and anger

Intrusion into family and private life is rarely welcomed, and service users may be reluctant to express the extent of their needs or even ask for information and clarification. On the other hand, they may be scared or distrustful, which can lead to resistance, silence or anger and aggression. In some instances, as will be discussed in Chapter 7, service users engage in deliberate deception.

Exercise 6.9: Practice reflection

Consider a recent social work situation in which you experienced a service user's hostility or resistance. Alternatively, consider some of the following examples of when a person:

- responds to you with shrugs or monosyllabic words;
- says that everything is fine, when their non-verbal language suggests this may not be true;
- shouts at you, and walks out or tells you to leave;
- agrees to appointments but does not keep them.

Think about what form these situations take, and how they can make you feel.

Resistance and hostility are very challenging to deal with; yet, in these situations good communication skills – including empathy, active listening and observation – are vital. Consider the following brief scenario.

Practice example 6.1

Mike and Stephen are a couple in their 50s, recently retired from senior management roles. Due to multiple sclerosis, Mike's mobility is now severely reduced and Stephen has become his full-time carer. A referral from the GP, apparently with the couple's permission, says that Stephen is being treated for severe depression and not coping well. When you visit, Mike does not say much but looks well cared for. Their home is smart and well-kempt. Stephen expresses regret that the GP has called you unnecessarily, and assures you that everything is fine and there is no need for any help.

On face value, this seems straightforward: the GP might have misjudged the situation, or things have improved. On the other hand, a wide range of contextual issues may impact on communication, such as whether the person has chosen to seek social work support or not; the level of risk and urgency perceived by both social worker and service user or carer; as well as factors related to power imbalances. This is a good example of when a social worker needs to use critical awareness, drawing on their professional knowledge and experience to 'tune in' to the particular situation. With no tangible safeguarding concerns that might trigger interventions against Mike and Stephen's wishes, the social worker might very likely respond by advising Stephen about the support available for carers and closing the case. Alternatively, the social worker may look for a way to 'leave the door open' and follow up this first contact.

Many writers emphasize the importance of social workers understanding the interrelatedness between their personal and professional selves (Ruch et al. 2010; Akhtar 2013). Gast and Bailey (2014) suggest that this interplay between the public and private selves – of both the worker and the service user – comes under strain in situations of resistance or reluctance. Practice Example 6.1, for instance, might arouse a social worker's anxiety about their own care relationships; they might feel inexperienced in working with a same-sex couple or feel intimidated by the couple's middle-class assertiveness and apparent affluence. At the same time, tensions between Stephen and Mike's public and private selves might make it difficult for them to ask for help. Thus, a complex set of dynamics is set in play, and the social worker needs to consider different hypotheses about what is going on.

In situations of high risk – investigating concerns about neglect or abuse, or where there is a need to immediately protect a child or vulnerable adult – social workers have to persist in engaging with the service user despite resistance. While it can be challenging to remain non-judgemental, empathy, as we saw earlier, is more likely to overcome resistance than an authoritarian or procedural approach (Forrester et al. 2008). Some practitioners find motivational interviewing, discussed in Chapter 5, a helpful approach where resistance involves ambivalence about change.

Resistance can become aggression, especially when a person is scared or feels they are not being heard. According to Koprowska (2014), hostility and aggression encompass behaviours that are verbally or physically threatening: swearing, using abusive language, shouting, making physical assaults and preventing a person from leaving.

Exercise 6.10: Aggression

Consider the following fictional conversation where social worker Rick is faced with an angry parent and then answer the following questions:

- Why do you think Kevin and Nancy might be acting the way they do? Try to think of at least two different explanations.
- Who has power in this scenario?

- Write some feedback for Rick about which aspects of his practice have helped and hindered communication.

Rick is supporting a family whose three-year-old son is the subject of a child in need plan. Luke is very behind in his speech and general development, and his parents, Kevin and Nancy, are not consistently taking him to nursery or for health appointments. Kevin and Nancy are also finding it difficult to manage their son's tantrums. They are both out of work and struggling with debt and poor housing in a third-floor rented flat. The family has recently acquired a dog, which is not yet house-trained, and on recent visits Rick has found dog faeces on the floor, which he has asked Kevin and Nancy to clear up. Kevin opens the door, makes a derogatory comment and leaves Rick standing on the doorstep. Nancy appears and leads Rick into the sparsely furnished living room, where Luke sits on the floor playing with toy cars. There is some 'small talk' regarding the weather, the dog and the toys with which Luke is playing.

Rick: So, how's the cleaning up going?

Nancy: Well, we did clear up all the dog poo. But with the weather being so bad, we can't take the dog out much and she has pooed everywhere again. So, we're going to shut her in the bathroom and start again this week.

Rick: OK, well, that's getting urgent now. It's not good for Luke to be playing with all that mess around, is it? It's rather smelly too. Are you committed to keeping the dog?

Nancy: Well, yes [silence]. I suppose my sister might be able to take her for a while and get her house trained.

Rick: OK, that's good. I would sort that out with her urgently, then.

Nancy: Yeah. As long as Kevin . . .

[Kevin comes into the living room looking tense. He stands next to Nancy's chair.]

Rick: So, Kevin, Nancy and I were talking about how things are progressing with cleaning up the flat and making sure Luke gets to nursery.

Kevin: [speaking in a loud and aggressive tone, punctuating his words with swearing] Look, Rick, I been talking to a solicitor and I'm not prepared to talk to you any more. Not after the way you accused me of neglecting Luke last week. You got no right to come in here and do that.

Rick: No one is accusing you, Kevin, but it's my job to make sure Luke is getting all the support he needs from . . .

Kevin: [shouting and swearing] You social workers just want to take children away. You got no right to come noseying around.

Rick: Now Kevin, that's not true at all. I explained to you last week why I'm here, but I don't think you're listening to me, are you?

(Adapted from 'Protecting Our Children', Episode 3 (2012). [TV programme] BBC Bristol).

You probably came up with one or two hypotheses to explain the resistance and hostility in this scenario. There is likely to be fear on both sides, and Rick may not feel as powerful as Nancy and Kevin perceive him to be (even though, objectively, he does have a lot of organizational and personal power). You might have suggested to Rick some things that he could do to minimize the risk of aggressive behaviour. One strategy is to be well-prepared when meeting service users: this is not only a matter of reading case records before a first visit, but also continuing to reflect on the family's situation in the light of your theoretical knowledge about possible psychological, social and biomedical explanations for the aggressive behaviour. Planning includes thinking about how potentially sensitive topics might be introduced and discussed. Effective communication skills can often prevent threatening situations from arising in the first place. Kevin and Nancy are clearly struggling with some difficult economic and family circumstances. Even in situations where social workers need to be assertive and authoritative, drawing on the core conditions and values of respect and honesty can go a long way to defuse conflict, along with showing empathy and being as non-judgemental as possible.

Research note: Responding to signs of aggression

Koprowska (2014) summarizes expert advice for responding to signs of aggression:

- Take an assertive, confident approach (without being authoritarian).
- Use the person's name to help make a personal connection.
- Name the behaviour (be specific and descriptive, say what impact it has on you and ask the person to stop).
- Avoid addressing the person's issue until the aggressive behaviour has stopped (or consider changing the subject).
- Avoid using the word 'please' except in the middle of an utterance (this can sound too pleading).

Koprowska notes conflicting advice about the use of questions when a person has become aggressive. Braithwaite (2001, cited by Koprowska) recommends using statements rather than questions until the aggressive behaviour has stopped. Others, however, suggest using open questions about how the person thinks the situation can be resolved, what is causing their anger and what you can do to help.

While preparation and good communication skills can prevent aggression from escalating, it is nevertheless important for social workers and their managers to take personal safety seriously. Your employer should have guidance in place to protect social workers, and policies to support staff who have experienced violence or fear-provoking incidents. As a matter of professionalism, the individual social worker also has a responsibility for seeking supervision when an aggressive incident has taken place or is a possible risk.

Exercise 6.11: Defusing anger

Looking at the guidelines in the Research note, which of the following responses would you choose to try and defuse an angry situation such as the one faced by Rick?

- 'Behaving like this is going to make things much worse for you'.
- 'Please don't do this, I'm only doing my job'.
- 'You're shouting very loudly, Kevin, and it's making me feel uncomfortable. Please sit down and then let's talk through what you're angry about'.

Koprowska's advice would suggest that the first response is too authoritarian, as well as vague, whereas the second response is both vague and too pleading. The third response is better because it is specific, uses the person's name and asks them to stop. It also demonstrates a willingness to respond to the issue once the behaviour has stopped. Returning to Rick, you may have commended his efforts to remain calm and assertive when faced with Kevin's anger. On the other hand, comparing this extract with Tracey and Sarah in Exercise 6.4, you may have questioned how well Rick conveys empathy and respect for the parents' perspectives.

Summary and conclusion

A range of complex communication scenarios have been explored in this chapter, each one highlighting the importance of using skills typically associated with professionalism to offer the best possible service to diverse service users. As you have seen, social workers must use their professional knowledge and power – guided by strong social work values – to select styles and methods of communicating that are as empowering as possible for each individual. As part of CPD, develop your repertoire of communication skills, keep abreast of research into best practice, and use supervision to enhance your criticality and emotional resilience.

Key points from this chapter

- Professionalism requires social workers to maintain a critically reflective approach towards their own communication skills, reviewed in the light of social work values and self-awareness about the professional use of power.
- When working with people whose verbal and/or cognitive skills are limited, effective communication is not only a matter of using specialist techniques – it is important also to critically engage with each situation and find creative, empowering ways to develop a professional relationship.
- Good communication skills and empathy are essential in contexts of resistance and hostility, along with self-awareness to maintain safety for yourself and service users.

Recommended reading

Adams, J. and Leshone, D. (2016) *Active Social Work with Children with Disabilities*. Northwich: Critical Publishing.

Gast, L. and Bailey, M. (2014) *Mastering Communication in Social Work: From Understanding to Doing*. London: Jessica Kingsley.

Koprowska, J. (2014) *Communication and Interpersonal Skills in Social Work*, 4th edn. London: Sage.

Lefevre, M. (2010) *Communicating with Children and Young People*. Bristol: Policy Press.

Woodcock Ross, J. (2016) *Specialist Communication Skills for Social Workers*, 2nd edn. London: Palgrave Macmillan.

The following websites are a useful source of specialist advice and tips:

- Community Care: Tips for social workers: Working with interpreters in mental health: http://www.communitycare.co.uk/blogs/childrens-services-blog/2012/06/working-with- interpreters/#.WaWpM7KGO1s
- Community Care: Top tips for working with independent advocates: http://www.communitycare.co.uk/2017/02/07/top-tips-working-independent-advocates/
- Motivational interviewing: http://www.stephenrollnick.com/
- NSPCC: Solution-focused practice toolkit: https://www.nspcc.org.uk/services-and-resources/research-and-resources/2015/solution-focused-practice-toolkit/
- SCIE: E-learning resources on a range of communication skills and topics: http://www.scie.org.uk/publications/elearning/communicationskills/
- SCIE: E-learning resources on dementia communication: https://www.scie.org.uk/dementia/advanced-dementia-and-end-of-life-care/advanced-dementia/communication.asp

7 Safeguarding and risk management skills

Chapter overview

By the end of this chapter, you will:

- Understand the importance of a constructive working relationship
- Know the advantages and disadvantages of using structured risk assessment procedures and tools to assess risk
- Understand how critical analysis and analytical tools can support social workers to evidence their thinking and avoid bias

Introduction

When concerns arise about safeguarding, social workers find themselves engaged in a statutory framework of procedures, and confidence is needed to bring their own blend of professional self and skills to bear. Nuanced judgements about risk and how to respond to risk cannot be made simply through applying procedures. Professionalism – informed by professional values, theoretical and research insights, and critical reflection – is thus especially important in this area of social work.

This chapter focuses on assessing risk, using the professional relationship, and critical reflection and analysis. These were highlighted in Munro's (2011) final report on child protection, and are increasingly recognized as essential in safeguarding work with adults. Whatever your current level of experience, this chapter invites you to review and reflect on your skills via practice examples. As you do so, keep in mind the underpinning professional capabilities outlined in Chapter 4. We discuss what the research says about using structured risk assessment tools and protocols, and then look at some less formal tools that can be used to support your own critical analysis. This chapter does not discuss the specific legislation and guidance that sets out expectations and processes for responding to safeguarding concerns, but provides a list of further reading and resources.

Concepts of safeguarding and risk in social work

There are some important legal and contextual differences when managing risk and safeguarding for children as opposed to vulnerable adults. There are nevertheless many commonalities: child or adult, safeguarding legislation embodies the principle that *all people have the right to live full lives and achieve their potential, free from abuse and neglect.* In practice, the work of safeguarding places social workers in the position of exercising power and deciding how to balance control with care. Before examining skills, therefore, it is worth pausing to consider the difficult and emotionally-charged context in which safeguarding takes place.

The term 'safeguarding' refers not only to protecting children and vulnerable adults from harm, but more broadly to promoting individuals' welfare, health and development. In recent decades, however, the organizational focus has narrowed to managing the risk of harm, arguably at the expense of social work's concern with responding to people's welfare needs within a social justice framework (Barry 2007; Kemshall 2013). This has led to the development of extensive systems and procedures that attempt to predict and manage risk (Webb 2006). And yet, as experienced social workers know, risk and harm are relative concepts and cannot be fully predicted or prevented (Taylor 2013). At best, it is only possible to reduce the *probability* of harm.

Risk itself is a difficult concept to define. Different professional groups do not necessarily perceive risk in the same way (Barry 2007). Not only that, but practitioners and service users may have divergent views about what risk is, and often use different language to talk about it (Carr 2010; McLean 2017). This uncertainty opens up the potential for power differences to come into play when defining and assessing risk. Alaszewski and Alaszewski (2002), writing about people with learning disabilities, suggest that professional opinion carries more weight than service users' lived experience and that professionals tend to prioritize people's safety over their empowerment.

Organizational culture can impact on decisions about risk; lack of management support, for example, can lead to risk aversion rather than risk enablement (McLean 2017). In adult safeguarding, despite the emphasis of the Care Act 2014 on enablement, agency structures can give the impression that taking risks is to be avoided at all costs, rather than viewing it in its human context of everyday choices and rights. This conveys the message that people using services do not have the same 'right' as others to make 'risky' choices or unwise decisions.

Professional power can be shaped in response to public and media stereotypes about dangerous populations (Taylor 2013). Despite a gradual change in public attitudes, the assumption persists that users of mental health services present a risk to other people (TNS BMRB 2015). A review of research (Mitchell and Glendinning 2008) found that this influences professional decisions about capacity and competence. Additionally, Warner's (2006) research indicates that these assumptions can produce an inbuilt bias in risk assessment tools. For example, it has been suggested that stereotypes about sex, gender and race are the reason that black men using mental health services are more often assessed as violent and posing a risk than white users of the same service (Warner 2006; Ray et al. 2008).

Exercise 7.1: Views about risk

- What is your personal view about risk? Jot down one example of a risk to yourself that you see as 'acceptable' and one example of a risk you would find 'unacceptable'. What personal assumptions and values underpin this?
- If applicable, how does your personal approach compare with your organization's view?

Comparing readers' answers would reveal a range of tolerances for personal risk – willingness to holiday in a country that has a high terror threat level, for example. If you find this an acceptable risk to yourself, would you make the same decision on behalf of a child in your family? If the traveller were a looked-after child or a vulnerable adult, legislation, procedures and management culture would influence the organizational view of risk.

Another source of complexity for safeguarding work is the heightened emotional context for both social workers and service users. Where individuals are at risk, decisive action may need to be made quickly. Professionalism is needed to respond to people's immediate shock and distress, managing one's own feelings and being able to stand back and assess the events. Certain kinds of concern create personal and professional value dilemmas: when dealing with an adult's self-neglect, for example, social workers have to balance the human right to autonomy and self-determination with the legal duty to protect health and well-being.

Gathering sufficient and accurate information about actual or potential harm and neglect can be extremely difficult. Complex family dynamics may not be immediately obvious, which can make it difficult to gain a rounded understanding of the situation. Mitchell and Glendinning's (2008) review of research found that both service users and practitioners can be reluctant to share risk-related information. Social workers may be trying to gather information from people who are scared (and even being coerced), and there may be deliberate attempts to conceal information. When a person has communication and cognitive difficulties, it can be even harder to be sure what has happened. Gathering information from a number of professionals and agencies, social workers may have to reconcile fragmented and contradictory accounts.

What skills are important in safeguarding?

Exercise 7.2: Safeguarding skills in practice

With the challenges discussed in mind, consider the following practice examples.

- Create a list or diagram of the professional skills that might be needed by these two social workers to assess and work with the situation.

Practice example 7.1

Maureen and Paul (adapted from Jones and Watson 2013).

Helen, an experienced social worker, received a referral from a local GP requesting a care and support needs assessment for Maureen, a widowed lady aged 84 who showed early signs of Alzheimer's disease. Maureen had declined appointments with a dementia specialist, because she didn't want to leave her 50-year-old son alone. Paul had mild learning difficulties but, according to the GP, had attended mainstream school and never received any services. Maureen had, however, written to the GP saying that she needed help with Paul's care.

Attempting to arrange a meeting, Helen initially received no reply to her letters and phone calls. Eventually, Maureen answered the phone and told Helen that she didn't need any help. Although agency procedures would usually require the case to be closed, something in Maureen's hesitant way of speaking caused Helen to feel uneasy. She made several brief but friendly phone calls to Maureen over the next few weeks, and eventually a home visit was agreed.

Helen arrived at the house but got no reply. While she was re-checking the address, she caught a glimpse of a woman – presumably Maureen – peering from a window but, despite Helen's renewed knocking, the door remained unanswered. Helen was writing a note to put through the door when the next-door neighbour beckoned her over and suggested she try the side entrance, adding that 'Paul won't let her open the door to anyone' and that he had 'a very nasty temper, and will be the death of Maureen one of these days'. Helen tapped gently on the side door and Maureen invited her in.

Practice example 7.2

Kaylee (adapted from Saltiel 2013).

Kaylee, aged six months and suffering from vomiting, was brought to hospital by her father, Ryan. His partner, Nina, was at home with their other children, aged two and four. Medical investigations revealed retinal haemorrhaging (bleeding in the back wall of the eye), which raised concern about the possibility of non-accidental injury. Ryan could not offer any explanation and said that the baby had woken crying in the night and started vomiting soon afterwards.

Bilal, an experienced hospital social worker, was allocated to undertake an initial assessment. There had not been any previous social services involvement. In talking with other professionals, Bilal found that the health visitor was already quite concerned about the parents' care of the baby, who had been profoundly brain-damaged at birth. There were concerns about Kaylee's slow weight gain and her parents' difficulties in managing her nasogastric tube. Kaylee had missed a number of appointments with paediatric specialists and her parents did not seem to follow medical advice. Going to meet Ryan on the ward, Bilal was struck by how distraught he seemed to be by his daughter's condition, and Bilal sensed that Ryan was genuinely bewildered by the hospital's response. On hearing that Kaylee was being admitted overnight for medical treatment, Ryan agreed a home visit with Bilal and said he would go and explain everything to Nina.

Each scenario presents a potentially worrying set of circumstances. Is Maureen at risk of domestic abuse? Does Paul need help? Do Kaylee's parents understand her needs, and might she be at risk? As social workers, Helen and Bilal have a challenging task ahead of them.

Compare your ideas with the following list of skills, which we have created from the Knowledge and Skills Statements for adults and children in England (DfE 2015; DoH 2015). Helen and Bilal would need to engage with the families and start building trust and a working relationship. They could achieve this by:

- using clear and authoritative communication with the families and with the other professionals;
- gathering information to establish a fuller picture about what was happening;
- considering and analysing different kinds of information (about harm and risk indicators, about the family and about different perspectives within the family) and considering different hypotheses;
- critically reflecting on the situation in the light of theoretical and research knowledge;
- using supervision to discuss their findings and interpretations and develop plans for further intervention;
- managing their own emotional response (also sharing this in supervision);
- writing records and reports, and perhaps presenting reports to a case conference or similar forum;
- involving an advocate where service users may find it difficult to express their perspective;
- working collaboratively and sharing appropriate information with other agencies;
- alongside all of these, maintaining a constructive, non-judgemental and collaborative relationship with the family.

Some local safeguarding boards are incorporating recent practice developments that use a strengths-based and solutions-focused approach to assess risk and involve individuals and families in decision-making. *Signs of Safety®* (*SoS*; Resolutions Consultancy 2017) has been adopted – either wholesale or in modified form – by many agencies responsible for child protection work. In adult services, local authorities are expected to practise the 'outcome-focused' approach of the *Making Safeguarding Personal* (MSP) initiative – now embodied in the Care Act 2014 – when assessing and responding to allegations of risk (LGA 2018). What the two models have in common is a person-centred process that assesses both dangers and strengths, taking these into account when deciding what action is needed. The ultimate success of these models, however, relies on the social worker's relationship-building skills.

Using relationship-building skills in safeguarding

A key element of professionalism in safeguarding practice is to draw on social work values and communication skills (discussed in Chapter 6) to create a working relationship that combines care and control. Social workers need to know how to build trust with people who are scared, angry and resistant to social work intervention. You may feel this is easier said than done, and there is no doubt that creating trust in the face of resistant or hostile behaviour is challenging. Even more stressful for practitioners is when resistant behaviour might indicate deception, which itself may be due to fear of the consequences. Serious case reviews have been critical of social workers who failed to spot deception, but it is difficult to balance relationship-building with maintaining a healthy sense of scepticism. Research suggests that we tend to have a bias towards credulity, towards thinking someone is telling the truth (Koprowska 2014). Although the social work principle of being non-judgemental involves being empathic and respectful, it can also mean reserving judgement and keeping an open mind while systematically exploring what is happening. Ferguson (2011) argues for the ethical use of social work power and exercising 'good authority': by this he means being clear and honest with individuals and families about your concerns, while conveying empathy for their perspective and acting, as far as possible, in accordance with the principles of social justice.

A substantial body of research evidence highlights the benefits of relationship-building in statutory social work. Communicating openness to the individual's or family's perspective increases their engagement and reduces resistance, enabling social workers to gain a more thorough understanding of the situation and the family's needs and strengths (Turney et al. 2011). Evaluative research into *SoS* (Bunn 2013; Keddell 2014; Baginsky et al. 2017) highlights that the participatory approach enables individuals and families to feel respected, better understood and less blamed. The participatory process enables both practitioners and parents to believe that change is possible, and families are more likely to take part in generating outcomes and resolving difficulties. With adult safeguarding, research by Needham (2015) found that, whereas social workers had previously concentrated on establishing and verifying the details of the abuse, MSP prompted them to ask the person what they wanted the safeguarding process to achieve; for this reason, social workers felt more able to draw on professional values to work with people who are disadvantaged or marginalized. This is consistent with the improved relationships and outcomes reported by Lawson et al. (2014a) and Hopkinson et al. (2015).

Exercise 7.3: Reflection on relationship skills

Revisiting the case studies of either Maureen or Kaylee, consider the following questions:

- What might the social worker say or do to build a trusting relationship?
- What might the social worker be thinking and feeling about this situation?
- What issues would you advise the social worker to reflect on in supervision?

Now reflect on an example from your own practice:

- Think about a practice situation in which your relationship-building skills created positive change for a service user. What was it about your practice that made this difference?
- How did you use 'good authority' in the relationship, and what did you do to show both care and control?
- How did you use emotion (the service user's and your own) in gaining insight into the situation?
- Relationship skills are also an important aspect of inter-professional work. Now reflect on how you used your skills to build a productive relationship with another professional.

Munro (2011) highlights the importance of practitioners being able to read and understand their own emotional responses, and to use this self-awareness as a basis for understanding others. She suggests that on meeting a family, an experienced social worker quickly gets an intuitive awareness of the dynamics, the strength of relationships, or the level of fear felt by a child. Munro emphasizes, however, that intuitive understanding must be accompanied by objective, logical analysis of risk.

Assessing risk and making decisions

Assessing risk involves gathering the fullest possible information, which can be very challenging within the required timeframe. There is a substantial body of research about how social workers make decisions when assessing risk.

Research note: Risk assessment decisions

When social workers make risk assessment decisions, they integrate different kinds of knowledge: objective, procedural and theoretical knowledge, alongside an implicit store of practice-based knowledge or 'intuition' (Zeira and Rosen 2000: 104; Stokes and Schmidt 2012).

To make sense of this knowledge, alongside the information collected during the assessment process, social workers typically combine both analytical and intuitive reasoning. According to Munro (2011), research shows that our brains process data in two separate ways. Intuitive reasoning enables us to think quickly, drawing on emotion as well as the wealth of our knowledge and expertise. But it is also this that reflects biases, including stereotypical generalizations. In analytical thinking, our brains systematically work through a series of steps, but the process is slower. An experienced social worker's skilled use of intuition enables them to quickly tune in to nuances of behaviour and emotion in the family's situation (for example, visiting an individual or a family for the first time) and helps the social worker to prioritize what is most pressing. Their analytical mode kicks in as they begin the formal processes required by the visit.

Referrals about risk and harm trigger a set of procedures governed by national and local protocols. It has become part of the safeguarding role to follow a standardized framework, often guided by detailed forms and a wide range of structured risk assessment and decision-making tools designed for specific circumstances or settings. Procedures and tools can be a way of formulating best practice and reducing variations in the quality of service received (Munro 2011). There is, however, considerable debate about their usefulness.

Some risk assessment tools are based on an actuarial approach; that is, they have been developed from empirical evidence about the statistical probability of risk in different circumstances. There is a substantial body of evidence that actuarial models are able to predict abuse or neglect more accurately than 'clinical' or professional judgement alone (Taylor 2013; Wilkins 2015). Thus, standardized protocols are designed to guide decisions about what information is to be gathered, whose views should be obtained and (sometimes) the timescale for completing each step. Once the information has been gathered, there may be further tools that calculate the seriousness of the risk and the need for intervention. Structured tools and forms also provide a means of recording and auditing the decisions. Using these formal processes is said to address research findings that, when determining risk, practitioners draw on limited or conflicting data, often under organizational and political pressure, and that they are reluctant to change initial judgements (Munro 1999; Stokes and Schmidt 2012; Taylor 2013). Tools also help to minimize the personal bias that may influence a practitioner's judgements (Taylor 2013).

Critics argue that the design of structured tools encourages a fragmented and over-simplified depiction of complex situations at the referral stage (Broadhurst et al. 2010). Social workers have found that prescriptive paperwork, often involving tick boxes, does not cater for the complexity of what is happening in people's lives (Gillingham and Humphreys 2010). Linked with this, the time-consuming and administratively burdensome nature of the forms has been found to lead to errors, incomplete recording and the taking of shortcuts (Shaw *et al.* 2009; Broadhurst et al. 2010). Social workers can also find discrepancies between what the tool shows, the information they have gathered and their own feelings about what is happening in the situation (Gillingham and Humphreys 2010). An interesting – although unsurprising – finding from this research is that, whereas NQSWs tend to apply structured tools in the prescribed way, experienced workers are more likely to question their usefulness.

Exercise 7.4: Reflection on using structured tools and forms

- What kind of tools and forms have you used or studied for assessing risk?
- If you have been practising for a while, how has your approach to assessing risk changed with experience? If you are advanced in your studies, how have your views regarding risk assessment approaches changed?
- Where do you stand in the debate about standardized procedures and tools? If you have ever found the assessment process inflexible or unhelpful, how did you resolve this?

On balance, social work research seems to support the intelligent and flexible use of procedures and tools as an addition to professional expertise and judgement (Barlow et al. 2012; Taylor 2013; Wilkins 2015). Munro (2011) concluded that, although structured tools can provide a helpful framework, skill is needed to analyse and interpret the information gathered by these methods. Returning to the safeguarding referral concerning Kaylee: suppose that a structured risk assessment indicates she is not at risk, and yet Bilal is left with strong intuitive concerns based on the family relationships he has observed. Bilal would then need to critically reflect on all the evidence, preferably in supervision or with an experienced colleague, to form a more rounded analysis and consider whether more information is needed.

Strict timescales do not facilitate experienced practitioners making full use of their skills and expertise (Gillingham and Humphreys 2010). However, thanks to sector-led reviews (Munro 2011; Pike and Walsh 2015), timescales have begun to be relaxed, and there is increasing recognition of the professional skills needed to negotiate direct access to the child or adult concerned, visit people in their own homes, apply professional expertise and build a relationship in emotionally-fraught circumstances (Turnell and Edwards 1999).

The assessment methodology can make a big difference to how risk issues are perceived. Both the MSP and *SoS* approaches explicitly assess strengths as well as dangers, taking these into account when deciding what action is needed. Evaluations (Bunn 2013; Keddell 2014; Lawson et al. 2014a; Baginsky et al. 2017) indicate that social workers appreciate the models' simplified and flexible processes. While *SoS* is underpinned by a detailed theoretical and research knowledge, it uses a one-page assessment and planning form (Turnell and Murphy 2017) that is based on the following three areas of inquiry:

1. What are we worried about? (Past harm, future danger and complicating factors)
2. What's working well? (Existing strengths and safety)
3. What needs to happen? (Future safety)

A fourth area of inquiry uses the answers to these questions to rate the level of safety and seriousness on a scale of 1–10. As you can see from the example in Figure 7.1, although the form itself is simple, the assessment process is detailed and involves both family members and professionals. The anonymized and edited example shows how parents, Merinda and Eddy, worked with professionals from Australia's Child Protection Society (CPS) in response to safeguarding concerns about their children, Darel (aged 6), Alkira (aged 4) and Jirra (aged 18 months). The form also reflects the children's exact words from interviews.

An advantage of both MSP and *SoS* is their emphasis on actively and transparently engaging people in assessing the risks and strengths. The MSP model, for example, emphasizes 'having conversations' to explore how the adult perceives the risk and how they want it to be dealt with (Lawson et al. 2014b: 4). The *SoS* assessment protocol includes optional tools to elicit children's perspectives (discussed in Chapter 6), and some local authorities are beginning to adapt these methods to work with adults who have learning disabilities (Stanley 2016). MSP provides a clear process for responding to alleged risk and harm, but local authorities are free to design their own paperwork. One example – an *aide-mémoire* for practitioners – is shown in Figure 7.2

An important contextual difference between the two frameworks – reflecting societal expectations and legal principles about the balance of dependency and autonomy for children and adults – is that with *SoS*, social workers retain the authority to set acceptable parameters for progress and intervene where these are not met. In MSP, the principle of proportionality means that the person's wishes will be followed unless this puts another person at risk.

Exercise 7.5: Reflection on empowerment

Consider the case study of either Maureen or Kaylee.

- How might the principles used in the *SoS* or MSP approaches be used in an empowering way?
- In your view, would there be any disadvantages or issues?

Critically analysing risk and harm

Safeguarding assessment does not end with the completion of paperwork. Before decisions can be made, social workers need to apply critical analysis to the information that they have gathered. Critical analysis – or critical thinking – means adopting an open-minded, reflective approach that takes account of people's different perspectives, experiences and assumptions (Glaister 2008). This flexibility equips social workers to handle uncertainty, while working from a strong base of professional skills and knowledge. It can also help social workers to avoid bias in making decisions and to feel more confident about evidencing their thinking.

Signs of Safety® Assessment and Planning Framework

What are we Worried About?	What's Working Well?	What Needs to Happen?
Past Harm Merinda and Eddy both say that they have had lots of bad fights. CPS have heard about 21 separate fights between 16/10/2012 and 22/09/2013 with Darel, Alkira and Jirra nearby. On the 13/08/13 Darel called the Police saying that his mother had 'started up again'. When Police arrived, they found Darel, Alkira and Jirra crying and hiding in the bathroom. Merinda had rung Rose and Darel Snr to come and get the kids saying she was going to kill herself. In the last fight on 22/09/13, Eddy and Merinda were screaming and throwing things at each other. Merinda threw a glass of coke at Eddy, which hit the wall and smashed. Alkira badly cut her foot on the glass requiring stitches Sally and Diane talked to Darel and Alkira on 23/09/2013. Some of what they said was: • "When Mum and Dad are arguing, I take my sisters and we hide in the bathroom." • "Mum and Dad were fighting and smashed the glass that cut my foot. I was really crying. I had a big needle. I was brave." • "Mum shouts really loud and I don't want baby to die…because Mum stressing out, shouting and throwing things around." • "Mum was in the car and driving the wrong way, she tried to smash into Dad, Jirra was in the car. I thought she would get squashed." **Danger Statements** Sally and Diane from CPS are worried that when Merinda and Eddy fight they scream, shout, swear, throw things at each other, drive off dangerously with the kids in the car and Darel, Alkira and/or Jirra will be really upset and frightened and get hurt like on Tuesday night when Alkira cut her foot badly on a broken glass or end up in a really bad car accident and die. Sally and Diane are worried that Eddy and Merinda will hit the children when they misbehave and cause bruises or other injuries. Sally and Diane, Rose, Darel, Kerri and Pat are worried that Darel, Alkira and Jirra will think it is okay to scream, swear, throw things, hit, drive dangerously, threaten, punch or kick people, because of Merinda and Eddy's behaviour. If Darel, Alkira and Jirra do grow up doing these things they are more likely to have violent relationships, get into trouble with the Police and have the same problems in their future lives.	**Existing Strengths** Darel, Alkira and Jirra all get plenty of food and have good clothes, Darel is doing well at school and Alkira loves preschool, Jirra is on track developmentally. Darel and Alkira say they love playing football at the park with Dad and love playing hide and seek and building cubby houses with Mum. Merinda says she quit smoking weed two months ago and is not drinking alcohol after she went to Mum Rose's for a weekend. Eddy said that Merinda's strongwill helped her to do this. Merinda and Eddy have talked to Sally and Diane about what triggers their fighting and say they want to make changes. Merinda and Eddy would like to go to a couple/family type rehab place like the one in Wanneroo to help them change their ways. Rose and Darel live nearby and help the family a lot, looking after the children and can calm both Merinda and Eddy down when they are angry. Eddy and Merinda haven't had much contact with Eddy's parents Kerri and Pat. Kerri and Pat say now they are back in touch and know what has been happening they are willing to do whatever it takes to help Eddy, Merinda and the kids out. Eddy and Merinda say this would be good and they want the help. **Existing Safety** On 24/09/13, CPS and Police met with Merinda and Eddy and they made a plan to send the children to live with Rose and Darel so they could both work on their problems. Darel, Alkira and Jirra have been staying at Rose and Darel's since then.	**Safety Goals** Sally and Diane from CPS want Darel, Alkira and Jirra to be back with Merinda and Eddy because they all want to be together and there have been so many good times in their family. For this to happen they need Merinda and Eddy to work with Sally, Dianne and other people in their family to create a story that explains to Darel, Alkira and Jirra what all the worries have been about and why they went to stay with nana Rose. Once the story has been shared with the children Merinda and Eddy and the safety network will work with CPS to make a plan that the children can understand and shows everyone that: When Merinda and Eddy do argue they can sort things out without hitting or screaming and so none of the kids get scared: • Darel, Alkira and Jirra will only be in the car with Merinda and/or Eddy when they are safe to drive • Eddy and Merinda have ways of telling the kids off without punching, hitting and screaming at them • CPS will close the case when the safety plan has been working for 6 months after Darel, Alkira and Jirra go home. **Next Steps** Merinda and Eddy say they will stick to the safety plan and not visit the kids together. At the next meeting on Monday Dianne and Sally will talk with Eddy and Merinda about creating an explanation for the kids about why they can't live with Eddy and Merinda at the moment. Over the next two weeks they will work together to create a full words and pictures story for the kids. After the words and picture story is finished Sally and Diane will help Eddy and Merinda and the safety network work on a long-term safety plan.

Safety Scale: On a scale of 0 to 10 where 10 means, even if Merinda and Eddy do get stressed, angry and drink too much, everyone including the children know what Eddy, Miranda and the support people will do so no one gets screamed at, hit or scared and there's adults Darel, Alkira and Jirra can call and will come if they are worried and 0 means there's no plan to keep the kids safe when things start getting bad so the children can't be living with Eddy and Miranda right now, where would you rate the situation today?

0 ⟷ **10**

Figure 7.1 *Signs of Safety* assessment and planning form

Source: Turnell and Murphy (2017).

Outcomes the person may want to achieve from safeguarding
(Discuss and encourage the person to consider their top three outcomes)

1. I want the abuse to stop and to feel safe
2. I want help to protect myself in future
3. I want help to feel more confident
4. I want to be involved in what happens next
5. I want people involved in my case to do what they say they will do
6. I want the police to prosecute
7. I want help to access any support that may be available to me
8. Other

Alert Stage: Actions (Record on AIS and spreadsheet)	**Discussion to Include:**
• Meet service user/representative and have a face-to-face conversation • Consider mental capacity and complete a mental capacity assessment if appropriate • Give user/representative MSP leaflet with your contact details on • Explain safeguarding process • Identify suitable person to provide support, if required, it may be an advocate/IMCA • Consider Family Group Conference to help service user obtain outcomes • Record conversation with service user to include assessment of capacity and service user wishes • Record alert as per departmental guidance • Records should remain factual	• What is important to the service user. Have a conversation to help the service user to identify their top three priorities, and encourage the person to record them in a leaflet • What could be done to help the service user feel safer • What the service user wants to happen as a result of safeguarding (Outcomes) • What the service user doesn't want to happen • What help and support is needed to help the service user understand the process and express their views • What will happen next

Figure 7.2 Making safeguarding personal – *aide-mémoire* for practitioners
Source: LGA (2014: 17).

Critical analysis is essential for any kind of decision-making in social work, but research reveals recurrent concerns about social workers' shortcomings in this skill (Munro 1999; Turney 2014). Serious Case Reviews (SCRs) also highlight social workers' failure to show sufficient curiosity and dig deeper into complex situations, instead taking explanations at face value.

Thinking back to the first practice example of Helen and Maureen, what is noticeable is the social worker's persistence to explore a hunch rather than simply close the case at the referral stage. This was not just 'intuition': Helen's hunch was a product of her experience and her willingness to take a critical stance. As an experienced professional, it's likely that she used reflective supervision to analyse the situation in the light of professional values, theoretical knowledge and research evidence. Discussing options in professional supervision can help social workers to mobilize or develop their skills and knowledge in a creative way. In adult safeguarding, for example, Romeo (2015) encourages social workers to consider a wide range of skills, theories and techniques. She suggests that attachment-based approaches, family systemic work, solution-focused approaches and therapeutic skills can be as relevant to safeguarding work with adults as with children and young people.

Analytical tools for social workers

A number of frameworks have been developed to help social workers apply their analysis skills to decision-making (Dalzell and Sawyer 2011; Brown et al. 2012; Wilkins and Boahen 2013). Here, we consider three analytical tools. These are distinct from the risk assessment tools discussed earlier in that they are flexible and do not usually feature in formal procedures. It is also worth adding the 'health warning' that analytical models are designed to *aid* the thinking process, rather than to obviate the need for professional judgement and supervision. This is where your own professionalism will come into play, and where you will bring your professional values to the analysis along with your knowledge and skills. Thus, you will notice that two of the analytical tools are explicitly underpinned by the same value base and commitment to social justice that underpin practice.

To bring each analytical tool to life and help you think about how you might use or adapt it to support your day-to-day practice, each one is accompanied by some reflective questions. (There will be an opportunity for more detailed practice in Chapter 9).

Anchor (five-question framework)

The first approach is Brown and colleagues' (2012: 30) 'Anchor' framework for stimulating thinking when undertaking any kind of assessment. This very practical framework, which 'anchors' the assessment within an analytical context, incorporates five key questions:

- *What is the assessment for?*
- *What is the story?*
- *What does the story mean?*
- *What needs to happen?*
- *How will we know we are making progress?*

These questions are not intended as a checklist or to replace formal recording templates, but are designed to promote the quality of analysis for decision-making.

The first question prompts clarity and transparency about why an assessment is being undertaken, helping everyone to focus on the most relevant issues. The concept of a 'story' promotes a holistic exploration of the person in the context of their wider history and often requires making sense of, and sometimes challenging, different perspectives. This stage can incorporate visual tools such as genograms. Asking 'What does the story mean?' encourages the social worker to spend some time analysing the information and empathically thinking about what it means for the service user. This stage can also help the social worker to articulate and evidence the rationale for their professional judgement. The final two questions relate to planning and review. An important aspect of Brown and colleagues' model is its cyclical approach, which takes account of new information that comes to light, perhaps having tested out a hypothesis. Hence, second and subsequent cycles ask amended questions (Brown et al. 2012: 46):

- *What is the assessment for now?*
- *What is the updated story?*
- *What does the updated story mean?*
  - *Have the identified needs changed or do they need updating?*
- *What needs to happen in relation to the updated story?*
  - *Have specified outcomes been achieved? If not, why not?*
  - *Do we need to set outcomes for outstanding needs?*
  - *Was it the wrong outcome?*
  - *Was the work to deliver the plan the wrong work?*
- *How will we know we are making progress?*

Exercise 7.6: Brief reflection on the Anchor approach

Consider the following case of Samuel Alexander, summarized from press reports of an SCR (*Daily Telegraph* 2010; Dunning 2011; Cole 2012).

In 2010, 70-year-old Samuel Alexander, a man with complex healthcare needs, was murdered by his 22-year-old son, Mark. Samuel had been in receipt of direct payments and was being funded £945 per month for four personal assistants, although after his death no evidence could be produced that they ever existed. Mark continued to draw the payments after his father died, and it was never discovered where the money had gone.

The police investigation team were praised for their professionalism in painstakingly reconstructing the lives of the father and son. In describing the family context, the press reports described Samuel, a retired university lecturer, as cantankerous and indicated that he was a controlling parent. Proud of, and very ambitious for, his son – who had been offered a place at a prestigious university – Samuel was reported to have sought to prevent Mark from living with his girlfriend. The news reports suggested that Mark and his father, living together in the same house, were isolated within their neighbourhood.

The complexity of the family situation does not appear to have been known to the local authority. Indeed, the SCR criticized social workers' failure to monitor the appropriateness of the care arrangements or review Samuel's needs, and observed that their role seemed to be reduced to giving administrative approval.

- Imagine how using the Anchor approach might have made a difference to this outcome.

Three Domains of Critical Practice

The second tool is Barnett's (1997) model of critical practice (described by Glaister 2008), which can be used in any kind of social work to prompt a wide-ranging critical analysis of a person's situation. Encouraging social workers to take an open-minded and enquiring approach to their practice, this model is explicitly rooted in a value base that respects others as equals. It also takes a constructivist approach, viewing meanings as socially constructed.

Barnett breaks down the concept of critical practice into three areas or domains:

- **Critical analysis:** focused around professional knowledge
- **Critical action:** focused around professional skills
- **Critical reflexivity:** focused around professional values and self-awareness

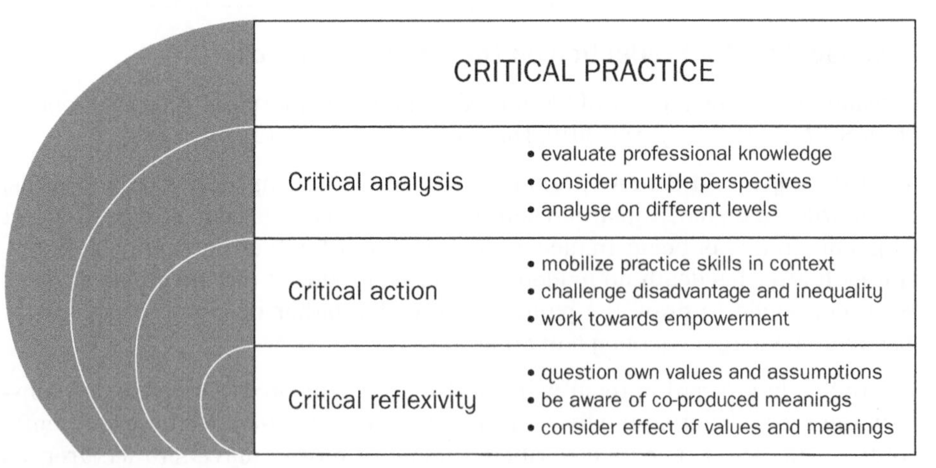

Figure 7.3 Three Domains of Critical Practice

Source: Adapted from Barnett (1997) and Glaister (2008).

The domain of critical analysis involves evaluating a situation in relation to professional knowledge (research and other evidence, policies and practice), taking account of multiple perspectives. Looking at the situation in terms of critical action, this part of the analysis is concerned with mobilizing professional skills to work towards empowerment, having regard to the structural disadvantage and power inequalities that impact on people's lives. Critical reflexivity, the third domain, proceeds from the premise that meaning is jointly produced between the worker and the service user, and thus invites social workers to scrutinize their own values and assumptions and consider what impact these might have on the situation.

To develop these ideas into an analytical tool, we have generated a set of reflective questions, which incorporate additional ideas from Dalzell and Sawyer (2011) and Fook (2015).

Three Domains of Critical Practice: reflective tool

Critical analysis: knowledge (research, theory, policies and practice) that throws light on the situation.

- What theories and research are relevant, and what do they tell me?
- Are there conflicting/different perspectives?
- What do policies and practice wisdom say?

Critical action: the wider social context and its impact on the situation.

- What elements of structural disadvantage (such as poverty, disability or culture) are relevant, and can their effect be modified?
- Are there conflicting or missing perspectives?
- Who has power, and how is it manifested?

Critical reflexivity: what you bring to this situation.

- What do I know or expect about this person's culture, gender, age, etc.?
- What stereotypes and prejudices do I hold (both positive and negative), and what are my values and assumptions?
- How might this person or family perceive me and my employer?
- What agency norms/practices and concepts do I take into this situation (risk thresholds, standards of parenting, etc.)?
- How does my presence/involvement influence the situation?
- What impact might my assessment have on the person or family's life and their perception of their life?
- What personal emotions and experiences might cause me to see the situation in a biased way?
- What power do I have in this situation?
- What is my gut feeling/intuition, and what alternative evidence do I need to consider?

Exercise 7.7: Brief reflection on the Three Domains

Read through the following real-life case (Oxfordshire Safeguarding Children Board 2016).

Child J, aged 17, was murdered by her 22-year-old ex-boyfriend in December 2013 after she told him she was pregnant with his child. Child J had been involved with social services and other agencies for several years and was known to be vulnerable, experiencing a range of significant family and mental health issues as well as poor school attendance. At the time of her death, she had presented herself as homeless and been placed by social services in supported accommodation. It was known that her ex-boyfriend continued to be abusive, controlling and violent towards her. Despite this, according to the SCR, social workers and other agencies treated her as a difficult young adult rather than as a vulnerable child needing protection. There was a tendency to focus on a series of individual crises experienced by Child J, rather than her overall circumstances.

- Consider how using the Three Domains might have made a difference here.

Decision tree

The final analytical tool is the decision tree, described by Wilkins and Boahen (2013). A decision tree can support social workers to weigh up the potential

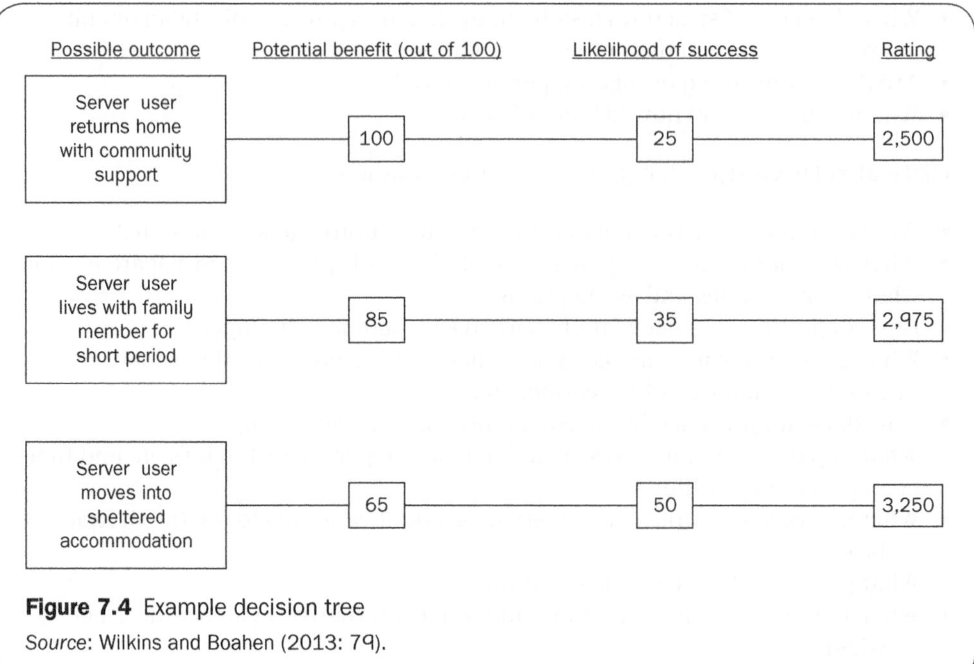

Figure 7.4 Example decision tree

Source: Wilkins and Boahen (2013: 79).

impact of different courses of action, and can be used to aid clear thinking even when not directly leading to a decision. Using a decision tree can also highlight gaps in existing knowledge.

The diagram in Figure 7.4 was developed using a word processor, but can equally well be handwritten.

1. The first step is to identify and list all the possible options for the service user – have a look at Figure 7.4 for an example of how to lay these out.
2. Next, evaluate the potential benefit of each option (ideally in partnership with the service user) and assign a numerical value between 0 and 100. For example, if a service user wishes to return from hospital to their own home, this might be rated as 100, whereas moving into supported accommodation might be 65.
3. Now, evaluate the likelihood of each option being successfully achieved: returning home might only score 25, while the supported accommodation option might be 50.
4. Finally, for each option, you multiply the potential benefit and the likelihood for success. In our example, returning home has an overall rating of 2,500, whereas supported accommodation rates 3,250.

Clearly, this is a subjective process and its value lies in the thinking process that goes into it; it certainly should not mean that the decision is mechanistically removed from the service user. While decision trees will not appeal to every social worker, they can be a useful conceptual tool to promote discussion about different possibilities, the rationale for recommending one option over another and – equally valuable – what action might be needed to increase the likelihood of success for the preferred option.

Exercise 7.8: Brief reflection on decision trees

Create a decision tree to weigh up some personal options that you are currently considering. It may be that you are trying to plan an event or holiday that will appeal to a diverse group of family or friends, or you may even be faced with a major life decision such as a potential career change.

Summary and conclusion

This chapter has considered professionalism skills in relation to safeguarding. In particular, we have discussed ways in which constructive social work relationships, underpinned by professional values and the appropriate use of professional power, can strengthen the safeguarding process and be more empowering for the service users concerned. We have also considered how formal procedures and protocols can be used intelligently alongside professional judgement. This cannot be achieved without using the skills of critical analysis with reflective professional supervision, which enable social workers to integrate their professional knowledge with practice wisdom, values and research findings. Safeguarding is challenging and emotive work, but supervision can support social workers' emotional resilience. Finally, professionalism is needed to continually develop relationship-building skills and keep abreast of new knowledge and research.

Key points from this chapter

- Social workers need to use their professional skills and values to combine care and control within the safeguarding relationship, building trust even when people are resistant to intervention.
- Openness to service users' perspectives increases their engagement in finding solutions and creating change.
- There are both advantages and disadvantages of using structured risk assessment procedures and tools; but, on balance, the intelligent and flexible use of a standardized process is considered helpful when used alongside professional expertise and judgement.
- Critical analysis equips social workers to handle uncertainty, working from a strong base of professional skills and knowledge. Analytic tools do not replace professional judgement or reflective supervision, but they can support social workers to evidence their thinking and avoid bias in making decisions.

Recommended reading

Cooper, B., Gordon, J. and Rixon, A. (2015) *Best Practice with Children and Families: Critical Social Work Stories*. Basingstoke: Palgrave Macmillan.

Ferguson, H. (2011) *Child Protection Practice*. Basingstoke: Palgrave Macmillan.

Jones, K. and Watson, S. (2013) *Best Practice with Older People: Social Work Stories*. Basingstoke: Palgrave Macmillan.

Taylor, B. (2013) *Professional Decision Making and Risk in Social Work*, 2nd edn. London: Sage.

Wilkins, D. and Boahen, G. (2013) *Critical Analysis Skills for Social Workers*. Maidenhead: Open University Press.

The following websites contain useful resources and research:

- Making Safeguarding Personal: https://www.local.gov.uk/topics/social-care-health-and-integration/adult-social-care/making-safeguarding-personal
- *Signs of Safety*®: https://www.signsofsafety.net/

8 Leadership skills

Chapter overview

By the end of this chapter, you will:

- Know the definitions of leadership and management
- Be able to explain theoretical models of leadership applicable to social work
- Understand how models of leadership apply to everyday practice
- Be able to critically reflect on issues of diversity and ethics in leadership

Introduction

In this chapter, we discuss leadership skills, which are increasingly considered to be an important indicator of the professionalism of social workers (The College of Social Work 2015). We explore models and theories of leadership and show how social workers can acquire the accompanying skills and adopt them in their practice. The social work literature on leadership is drawn from the wider body of work in management, administration and sometimes the military (Peters 2017). Therefore, we will survey the broader theoretical landscape before exploring some models of leadership pertinent to social work. We then move on to explain leadership skills in social work. Our focus remains the development of the requisite leadership skills, and so we provide examples and exercises throughout the chapter. First, we want to demystify the cult status given to leadership by explaining how social workers display leadership in everyday practice.

The context of leadership in social work

Leadership is the ability to effect change in people, organizations or situations. Peters (2017) explains that:

> Social work leadership can be preliminarily defined as a collection of organisational, relational, and individual behaviours that effect positive change in order to address client and societal challenges through emotional competence and the full acceptance, validation, and trust of all individuals as capable human beings (p. 10).

In everyday language, the word 'leader' typically conjures up an image of a person at the top of an organization's hierarchy who has power to direct others to accomplish a vision that they have developed. From the UK social work perspective, in keeping with managerialism, this latter conception of leadership is also propagated by policy-makers. It is claimed that statutory social work must be 'transformed', hence the need for authority figures to drive institutional changes (Lawler 2007). However, as Fairtlough (2017) has argued, this stance creates the impression that leadership is akin to a senior management position instead of being a skill set required for everyday practice. That said, in some countries, including England, leadership has been incorporated into practice standards. To illustrate further, Domain 9 of the Professional Capabilities Framework (PCF) is 'professional leadership' and the Knowledge and Skills Statements (KSS) for adult social work state a desired capability in 'professional ethics and leadership'. Therefore, in England, it can be argued that the PCF and the KSS have instigated a parallel direction of leadership in direct practice with service users alongside a policy agenda for organizational change.

In social work, leadership is conflated with formal titles and roles because of the hierarchical nature of the profession (Fairtlough 2017). However, leadership skills are required in everyday practice to achieve successful outcomes for service users. While there are many models of inter-professional working (Nancarrow et al. 2012), in each, social workers are required to work closely with other professionals from allied statutory agencies such as health and education (HM Government 2015) to achieve a shared purpose for families. Within these practice frameworks, social workers are required to coordinate the work of professionals, chair meetings, provide advice and manage relationships. Even within individual agencies, discrete work processes require some leadership skills. For instance, when conducting assessments or care planning, social workers liaise with different professionals and family members, communicate the purpose of the work clearly to families and colleagues, and are accountable for their work. Social workers routinely encounter complex issues in practice, which they address by using different leadership skills such as problem-solving, critical analysis and decision-making. Another way that social workers show leadership is by positively affecting their colleagues' work by making decisions, delegating work, motivating them and advocating for others (Cullen 2013).

We hope that through this discussion, we have achieved our two aims in the Introduction. First, that we have explained that, conceptually, leadership is a skill set and a formal role. Second, that we have shown that, in everyday practice, we all deploy leadership skills in ways that may not always be obvious to us. We now want to extend the learning further by inviting you to reflect on your leadership skills.

Exercise 8.1 draws our attention to important dimensions of leadership such as that it involves the exercise of power, there is usually a goal to attain and it is associated with distinct skills. These will be discussed throughout this chapter, starting with an overview of the theories of leadership.

Theoretical overview

A helpful starting point for exploring the theories of leadership is to ask what a 'good' leader looks like. To answer this question, we draw on the work of Holroyd

Exercise 8.1: Reflection on practising leadership

In the Introduction, we explained how social workers draw on leadership skills in everyday practice. In this exercise, we invite you to reflect on situations in which either you have exercised leadership or you have observed leadership in action. Please use the points below as prompts for your reflection.

- Describe the situation.
- Identify the people involved – for instance, were they service users, colleagues or managers?
- What skills did you find useful?
- Explain the outcome of the leadership – was it beneficial?

(2015), who usefully summarized the development of leadership theory in chronological order. Holroyd's approach may be considered overly simplistic because it posits that these theoretical changes occurred sequentially when, in practice, they tended to build simultaneously on elements of each other, as we will see. Nevertheless, Holroyd's work is a useful analytical framework because it charts the changes in the conceptualization of leadership.

Holroyd notes that, initially, leadership theories focussed on personal qualities. Two strands of this were: a focus on the 'traits' or characteristics of good leaders and an analysis of their behaviours. Unsurprisingly, some of these were romanticized – for example, those considered to be heroes and thus great leaders were depicted as brave, charismatic and inspirational. These theories also led to debates about whether leadership skills were genetic or whether they could be learnt. Holroyd notes that a change in the direction and agenda of leadership theories occurred in the 1960s with the advent of contingency theories of leadership. Their central postulation was that different leadership styles were required for each situation – 'great' leaders were able to adapt accordingly, while others could not.

The 1970s saw a shift in attention from what leaders *do* to what they *did for their followers*. The important leadership theories of this period were servant leadership and transformational theories: 'transformational leaders tend to focus more on organizational objectives while servant leaders focus more on the people who are their followers' (Stone et al. 2004: 349). In both servant and transformational leadership, the leader considers the interest of the organization; however, in the former, the interest of the institution is prioritized, whereas in the latter, the leader considers the interest of members (employees) first. Currently, there is a re-focusing of leadership theories on the individual under charismatic leadership theories (Waldman et al. 2004). In Figure 8.1 we have illustrated the theoretical changes in leadership.

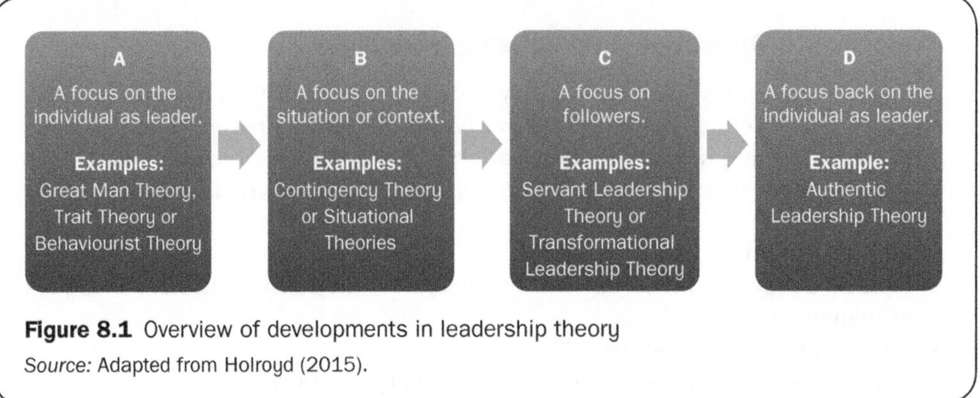

Figure 8.1 Overview of developments in leadership theory

Source: Adapted from Holroyd (2015).

Building on the preceding discussion, we now introduce an exercise designed to encourage you to reflect further on Figure 8.1.

Exercise 8.2: Identifying leaders

Try to identify one famous leader who conforms to the characteristics in A, B, C and D in Figure 8.1 (this can be a historical figure or current leader).

- A – Which leader is depicted as a 'Great Man' (or 'Great Woman') or someone who had unique leadership traits or behaviour in popular imagination?
- B – Which leader was faced with a crisis or challenging situation and managed this well?
- C – Can you name a leader who is said to have put the interest of their followers above their own?
- D – Which leader is deemed charismatic and 'authentic'?

Can you identify any commonalities between these leaders that you have selected (for instance, gender, class, race and/or ethnicity)?

This exercise invites us to consider leaders from popular culture and history. If you live in the Western world, it is likely that most of the leaders depicted in the mass media in your country are male, white, formally educated, middle class and in powerful positions. These leaders will also be portrayed as people who radically transformed their countries or companies. But, as we explain in the next paragraph, this understanding of leadership is criticized as gendered and implying the exertion of power by few people (Alvesson and Spicer 2012). These criticisms also extend to leadership theories – they tend to be preoccupied by the exercise of power and study figures from business, politics and the military, which are traditionally dominated by white men, despite there being great examples of leadership outside of this demography.

In leadership theory, it may be said that the present borrows from the past, hence our initial criticism of the model by Holroyd (2015). The research agenda has changed from understanding the individual characteristics of 'good' leaders to contextual factors of leadership (A–B). However, there is a return to focusing on individual leaders' characteristics alongside whether their followers accept their leadership. Furthermore, a more relational approach to leadership has emerged in contemporary leadership theories, with more attention paid to ethics and the disbursement of power in the leader–follower relationship (Avolio et al. 2009). In their literature review, Avolio et al. (2009) argued that contemporary models adopt a 'holistic' view of leadership, considering the skills of the leader, their followers and the contextual factors in the relationship. Current theories also postulate that leaders and their subordinates engage in a continuously-changing relationship in which power and influence move up and down the hierarchy. Let us examine this point further.

Leadership theories in social work

As we have discussed, there are many model of leadership.* In this section, we selectively present those models relevant to social work. In keeping with the overall *skills-based* approach of this book, we will explain the model of leadership and then provide a practice example. Our purpose here is to show how leadership is a necessary part of the toolkit of professionalism in social work, thus enabling readers to envision how each model can be replicated in practice.

Transactional leadership

In this model, the leader and their followers are engaged in exchanges that are mutually beneficial. The leader motivates their followers to perform for them (and, by extension, the organization) by outlining the rewards that they will gain if they are successful in the task. The leader, meanwhile, benefits from the 'transaction' because their stance enables their followers to meet organizational performance targets, which is their responsibility (McCleskey 2014). In our view, this is a model that a practitioner can draw upon to motivate people to change their behaviour. When we discussed motivational interviewing in Chapter 5, we explained that, before deciding to change people, consider whether the advantages of altering their behaviour are greater than the disadvantages. If it is on balance advantageous, then they are likely to change. Similarly, transactional leadership theory proposes that if the leader can explain to their 'followers' how the pros outweigh and cons of change, then they are likely to respond positively. We illustrate this point further with a practice example.

Practice example 8.1

In this example, you are a social worker for Mr Lombard, a 25-year-old man who lives in accommodation owned by the local authority. Mr Lombard was previously in the care of the local authority and is known to the police

* See Avolio et al. (2009) for a comprehensive overview.

for having frequent parties that lead to noise pollution. Mr Lombard also has parties in the week: this is a nuisance to families in his block of flats because their children are kept awake by the loud music and conversations. Due to his persistent offending, Mr Lombard has been informed by the local authority that he will be evicted. As his social worker, he has asked you to advocate on his behalf.

In this scenario, as the social worker, it is your interest that Mr Lombard is not evicted from his home because he will become homeless and probably more susceptible to risk of harm. It will also be beneficial to Mr Lombard to maintain his tenancy. Drawing on transactional leadership theory, you will explain to Mr Lombard the negative consequences of continuing his behaviour and the advantages of changing. To encourage him to modify his behaviour, you could inform him that you will advocate for him if he shows a willingness to change.

Transformational leadership

This is one of the most discussed models in the social work literature. In this model, the leader is at the apex of the organizational hierarchy and can convince subordinates to prioritize organizational needs ahead of their self-interest (Stone et al. 2004). Such leaders are interested in positive change, which they attain through communicating a vision to their employees and gaining their trust to achieve their goals. This model of leadership focuses on the skills and qualities of the leader – for instance, communication and analytical skills. Such leaders model 'good' conduct for their employees and take an active interest in their well-being.

Practice example 8.2

We can draw on a 'real' case scenario encountered by one of us (G.B.) in practice. G.B. worked with a 15-year-old young lady, Caroline, who was in the care of the local authority in a residential placement. Caroline came from a family of entrenched difficulties: her father was diagnosed with severe mental illness and her mother attempted suicide when she turned 16. Caroline regularly left her residential placement without informing staff, due to which she was reported as 'missing' to the police on several occasions. Caroline was also excluded from her school because of violence towards pupils and staff. Caroline distrusted adults and had a negative relationship with her family. This mistrust also extended to professionals, who she abused and refused to meet for her appointments. There was thus little coordination of Caroline's care.

Aspects of transformational leadership that could be deployed in the work with Caroline are:

- The social worker should form a trusting relationship with Caroline, involve her in care planning and, together, develop a plan to meet her life goals.
- The social worker can model good behaviour, based on trust and respect for Caroline. For instance, being punctual for meetings with Caroline, respecting her wishes, treating her as able to partake in decisions about her care, being courteous and showing moral character.
- The social worker can communicate an intervention plan to the professional network involved in Caroline's care and transform any negative perceptions of Caroline caused by her past behaviour.
- The social worker should display professionalism – they should be skilful in managing the complexities of the case, knowledgeable about the law and applicable theories, and seek specialist support for Caroline.

As you can see, aspects of transformational leadership are applicable in direct work with service users. However, this requires careful reflection because of the model's pre-eminent emphasis on the skills of the leader. In social work, there is an ethical requirement to respect and promote service users' self-determination. A second ethical requirement for social workers is the need to empower service users to make their own decisions instead of cajoling them to adhere to professionals' instructions. Additionally, the stress on the personal characteristics of the leader in transformational leadership divert attention from the relational and contextual factors that affect followers' performance (Peters 2017). For instance, Caroline had complex psychological, emotional and social care needs, which had to be addressed simultaneously. Without also assessing and meeting Caroline's emotional needs, the leadership skills of the social worker alone would not be enough for successful intervention.

Distributed leadership

In contrast to the two models discussed, distributed leadership places less emphasis on the personal attributes of the leader *as a person* and instead highlights the role of multiple actors in the *practice* of leading (Bolden 2011). Some of the characteristics of this model, identified by Bennett et al. (2003) as pertinent to social work, are that distributed leadership is an '*emergent property of a group or network of interacting individuals*' (p. 7; emphasis in the original), and the act of leading is open to more people. This means that, in this model, leadership is 'shared' within the group, enabling more members to participate in framing the group's direction. For this reason, in the literature this model is also called 'shared', 'collaborative' or 'participatory' leadership (Bolden 2011). There are overlaps between this and the partnership model that we discussed in Chapter 5 and they share similar skills with respect to professionalism.

Here we explain how social workers can equalize power with service users, as depicted by the model of distributed leadership. This equalization is important because it is also *ethical*.

Practice example 8.3

In this practice example, you are responding to the referral from a school about Anaya, who has a long-term medical condition. Anaya lives with her father, Mr Xavier, who describes himself as 'a quiet man' who wants professionals 'to tell me how to look after Anaya'.

In this practice scenario, Mr Xavier believes in the knowledge and skill of professionals and is willing to follow their instructions. However, this creates a risk of an unequal and unethical distribution of power in the relationship. To involve the family and encourage his participation, at the assessment stage practitioners can invite his involvement and encourage him and Anaya to describe her needs. Practitioners can also regularly consult them, formally and informally, during the review stages of any care plan. As the service users are particularly unwilling to challenge professionals' decisions, Anaya's social workers should refer the family to advocacy services to challenge the practitioners' decisions if there are disagreements. Another relatively straightforward way of sharing power with the family is by drawing their attention to the Complaints Procedure – through this, they will feel empowered to express any dissatisfaction with the service.

Servant leadership theory

In contrast to transformational leadership, in this model the leader prioritizes the interests of followers and their well-being over organizational interests. Advocates of this model emphasize the listening skills of the leader, through which they understand the issues problematic to their followers. The leader's motivation is to enable and empower others to succeed, and they achieve this through several skills. Examples include: encouraging subordinates to succeed, teaching them the requisite skills required to be successful and forming goals for their followers (Stone et al. 2004). In servant leadership, the leader also seeks to equalize power with their followers. They make themselves available to their followers, take direction from them, and seek to assist them to attain their goals including social justice and emancipation (Fields et al. 2015).

This model may be more familiar to social workers because their motivation to join the profession often stems from their desire to care for others, improve their well-being and empower them to fulfil their life goals (Clark 2006). Practice situations also require social workers to have emotional resolve and maintain belief in the human capacity to reform, even where service users have harmed other people.

Practice example 8.4

An illustrative practice example for servant leadership in social work concerns sex offenders. Cowburn (2000) discussed the frustration with this service user group because of their reluctance to confront the harm that they have caused to vulnerable people. Yet, placing their own emotions aside, social workers attempt to transform these service users. They do so by engaging with them, conducting keywork sessions with them during which details of their crimes may be disclosed, responding to their needs and wishes, and implementing care plans designed to change them.

The characteristic of servant leadership is the desire of the leader to put the needs of followers above their own. A similar model in this regard is leader–member exchange, which we will explore next.

Leader–member exchange

This model is referred to as 'LMX' in the literature and emphasizes the *quality* of relationship between the leader and their subordinates. The assumption is that both are engaged in a relationship of mutual exchange and that success for one also implies a gain for the other (Avolio et al. 2009). Consequently, the better the rapport between the two, the more likely they are to achieve their respective aims, and this in turn reinforces their relationship. Conceptually, this model is comparable to transactional leadership. The assumption is that the subordinates follow because they benefit from the leader, while the latter also gains from the relationship (Winkler 2009).

If we compare this description with the relationship between social workers and their managers, we can note several occasions of role reversal – for example, where the former recommends an action, which the latter must approve. Social workers know service users better than managers because they have more contact with them and their families, and often lead the work with them. It is therefore pertinent that the social worker and their manager have a good relationship because, that way, the manager would have quality information from the practitioner on which to base their decisions. The social worker, on the other hand, benefits from recognition and supportive management. The LMX leadership model is also applicable in direct practice – a good relationship between professionals and service users can be a conduit for achieving good outcomes (Ruch et al. 2010).

Practice example 8.5

Imagine two child safeguarding case scenarios, A and B, allocated to social worker Alex.

In scenario A, Alex has a transparent relationship with the family, who trust him and, as a result, feel safe to tell him about the routines in the home. During one conversation, Alex was informed by the children's mother that she sleeps with the baby on the sofa at night because 'Dad wants a good sleep before work'. Alex considered that there was a risk of cot death and he informed the family as such. Together, they developed a sleeping routine for the baby to minimize this risk.

In scenario B, in contrast, Alex and the child's parents have a strained relationship. They refuse to see him in their lawyer's absence because they believe that their case is now 'legal' and 'you will use whatever we tell you against us'.

We can see that, whereas Alex was able to assess the risk to the baby in family A, because of the quality of relationship, this would be more difficult to achieve in B (see Hingley-Jones and Ruch 2016). This shows that in certain situations, a good leadership outcome depends on the quality of relationship between the leader and their followers.

Summary

- We discussed selected models of leadership and created case scenarios to illustrate how aspects of these models can be adopted in practice.
- We showed the shift in substance agendas in leadership theory from a concern with *how* leaders exercise power and for *whom* — for instance, transactional and transformational models — to a current stress of democratic principles and diffusion of power — for instance, shared leadership and LMX.

Having provided the theoretical context, we will discuss management in social work in the next section. However, we first introduce an exercise to deepen your learning about the models discussed.

Exercise 8.3: Identifying your leadership style and skills

- Can you think of any leaders who correspond to the models that we have described? What are the reasons for your choices?
- Can you identify any unique skills required by each of the models? It may be helpful to separate these into people management skills and individual attributes.
- Out of the list that you have identified from the previous point, which do you think can be learnt and/or are innate?
- If applicable, reflecting on your own career history to date, what type of leader do you think you are?

Exercise 8.3 invites us to consider the specific skills associated with the models of leadership. Our view is that capabilities in leadership depend on the type of leadership style to which the social worker subscribes.

Skills for practising leadership

In Table 8.1, we present the leadership models and the skills required for their effective implementation in practice, based on our reading of the literature. Our position is that these skills can be learnt through training and CPD and are not necessarily attributes from birth, although some practitioners may have personalities that make them more conducive to adopting a particular model.

Table 8.1 Leadership models and skills map

Models of leadership	Associated skills
Transactional leadership	1. Verbal and written communication 2. Analysis and problem-solving 3. Emotional intelligence 4. Ability to empathize and understand other people's needs 5. Reflection
Transformational leadership	1. Communication 2. Ability to chair meetings and address an audience 3. Ability to form and outline a strategy 4. Capacity to motivate self and others 5. Ability to represent self and others 6. Knowledge and understanding of own area of responsibility
Distributed and participatory leadership	1. Teamworking 2. Chairing and overseeing meetings 3. Problem-solving 4. Ability to delegate and show accountability for work 5. Judgement and decision-making
Servant leadership	1. Prioritization and organizational skills 2. Ability to reflect on own position and outcome of interventions 3. Communication 4. Emotional resilience 5. Self-motivation and emotional intelligence 6. Advocacy 7. Self-leadership and understanding of own coping mechanisms
Leader–member exchange	1. Relationship-building 2. Communication 3. Ability to seek authority for work and be accountable for decisions 4. Critical analysis 5. Delegation

For instance, some people are more extroverted while others are more introverted – the latter may find it more difficult to address professional meetings or forums than the former. Some practitioners are also more inclined to take a strategic view about cases while others immerse themselves in the detail – this too may impact on the respective social workers' ability to communicate case direction.

Table 8.1 is not an exhaustive list of the skills associated with each leadership model, nor are they mutually exclusive to each model. We also want to restate the earlier point that the skills can be gained through training and CPD. Moreover, these skills are also required for the everyday management of cases, which we discuss next.

Management in social work

Management is about planning and organizing, considered to be a 'practical activity'; however, as readers can see from the previous discussion, leadership usually associated with *transformation* (Hafford-Letchfield 2010: 11). From this description, it could be argued that leadership and management imply a specific set of skills. The implication is that managers maintain the status quo whereas leaders are more likely to alter the way that organizations function. While this distinction may be conceptually valid, we argue that in social work practice there is a symbiosis of management and leadership qualities: in one sense we want to transform people's lives for the better, while also wanting to ensure stability by maintaining the routine parts of their lives, which are vital to their well-being. We will explore this point further in Exercise 8.4.

Exercise 8.4: Examining leadership and management in practice

Suppose a colleague has left your team and you have now been allocated one of their cases. It involves the Adnan family comprising mother Ivana (aged 32), twins Iso and Aisha (aged 12), and their brother Moses (aged 13). All the children have been diagnosed with global developmental delay (GDD) and are under the care of a local paediatric team. On being appointed their social worker, you re-analyse the case history and note the following:

- The children regularly miss appointments with the paediatric team.
- There are regular reports from the children's school that they are late, they seem hungry and they are untidy. The children have also frequently reported that they are kept up at night because of 'noise from that man'.
- The children have expressed a desire to have contact with their father, who lives in the same city.
- The children attend school via a taxi, which the local authority funds. This is due to concerns about their safety on public transport.

Identify the opportunities for leadership and management in this scenario.

The re-analysis in Exercise 8.4 indicates that the children's needs are complex, with indications that their mother requires support to manage them. This would require leadership skills such as communication (liaising with professionals involved with the family); constructing a plan to transform the family situation to make it more settled; and, if judged to be in their best interests, the social worker would need to respect the children's wishes to see their father and (re)introduce him into their lives. However, this case is not only about transforming the children's lives. There will be the need to manage all the taxi bookings because without this the children cannot attend school or any health appointments. These vulnerable children have been subject to instability in their lives, thus they will need their social worker to plan and organize their lives to maintain stability. Such stability would involve organizational, critical analysis and communication skills, all of which are associated with leadership.

Reflection point 8.1

We wish now to draw on the discussions in the preceding section to encourage you to consider the type of leaders in your organization (this can be your employment or educational institution) and leadership styles that you find favourable. The point of this exercise is for us to consider what makes a good leader and what they contribute to our work.

- *Begin by writing down the name of some of the leaders in your organization.*
- *How have these leaders influenced your everyday work? Can you identify any of their achievements?*
- *What are the personal and professional qualities that you admire in these leaders?*

The questions invite us to reflect on what good leaders contribute to social work organizations. Boehm and Yoels (2009) set out to ascertain the contribution of leadership style, worker empowerment and staff cohesion to organizational effectiveness. They found that worker empowerment was the most significant factor because it also led professionals to develop self-efficacy. As we show in Chapters 3 and 5, self-efficacy enhances the confidence of professionals and service users, thus fostering their creativity and motivation. Boehm and Yoels note:

> . . . social workers who feel professionally empowered have a sense of confidence and act more determinedly, thus promoting the different aspects of effectiveness. Those who are not empowered, in comparison, have less professional confidence and are more hesitant, and therefore they have difficulty bringing their actions to a successful conclusion.
>
> (2009: 1371)

What is surprising from this research, however, is that there was little correlation between organizational effectiveness and the leadership style. The researchers suggest that this may be because social workers are more committed to the needs of their clients than to the authority of their managers. If social workers are empowered, then they are motivated to meet their clients' needs, which also improves the organization's effectiveness. In similar research, designed to ascertain what accounted for good outcomes in a children's residential home, Hicks et al. (2009) found that, compared with level of expenditure, managers tended to have more impact. The researchers identified a possible cause of this positive impact to be managers ensuring consistent (high) levels of service, organizing their staff and resources, and engendering teamwork. Tafvelin et al. (2014) also found that where staff spent more time with their managers, this led to increased clarity about their roles and commitments. While the studies discussed here were based in different countries and social work settings, a common theme is that good leadership in social work is about managing professionals in a way that enables them to address service users' needs and not necessarily about creating a vision or managing change. A second implication of the research is that leadership in social work is distinct from that in other disciplines. Arguably, because social workers have clarity of purpose to serve others, this is an intrinsic motivation. Therefore, leadership roles turn on empowering these professionals to be creative and responsive to service users' needs.

Summary and conclusion

In this chapter, we have explored leadership and management skills in social work. From the beginning, we highlighted the recognition of leadership as part of the repertoire of skills required to demonstrate professionalism (Hafford-Letchfield 2010). We aimed to debunk the taken-for-granted notion that leadership in social work is associated with formal titles, roles or people's natural abilities. We have argued that social workers *practise* leadership in many domains of their work and, to this end, we explored models relevant to practice. In describing the models, we also highlighted changes in leadership theory, from a focus on individuals and their unique characteristics, to exploring contextual factors and, latterly, to concerns about leaders' democratic accountability and their ethical standpoints. Furthermore, we identified servant leadership as a model with which social workers may easily identify because they are motivated to serve and empower service users to attain their goals. However, we also showed that social workers can draw on aspects of all the models in their practice. For instance, elements of transformational leadership, with the theoretical emphasis on enabling change, can provide analytical problem-solving tools to manage complex and seemingly intractable cases. Similarly, aspects of distributed leadership can draw practitioners' attention to the need to respect service users' self-determination. In the second part of the chapter, we mapped out the distinct skills associated with each of the models, cautioning that they are not exhaustive and that there are some, for instance communication, that can be considered 'core' leadership skills.

Key points from this chapter

- There is a difference between leadership and management in social work. The former is about change; the latter is about organizing and maintaining successful existing arrangements.
- Social workers practise aspects of leadership in their roles. For instance, practitioners must communicate their plans to fellow professionals and service users, solve problems, make decisions and exercise judgement. They must also initiate positive transformation for service users.
- Understanding of leadership has changed from a focus on leaders' abilities to their democratic accountability and legitimacy.

Recommended reading

Lawler, J. and Hafford-Letchfield, T. (eds.) (2013) *Perspectives on Management and Leadership in Social Work*. London: Whiting & Birch.

9 Extended case examples

Chapter overview

By the end of this chapter, you will:

- Understand how to apply the approaches, tools and thinking of the preceding chapters to the extended case examples

Overview and how to use the case examples

The two extended case examples in this chapter will allow you the opportunity to apply some of the skills, ideas and tools that you considered in Chapters 3–9. The case examples are based on real-life situations, with names and other details changed to preserve anonymity and confidentiality. Between them, the case examples are relevant to four main areas of practice: older adults, child protection, adult safeguarding and people with learning difficulties. However, as they are based on real situations, other issues are interwoven such as mental health, domestic abuse and inter-agency communication. You will also find examples of different socio-economic circumstances and dilemmas, which may impact on service users' experiences.

Each case study is presented in stages, beginning with the referral information, and there are specific tasks for you to complete at each stage. Try not to get too preoccupied with the finer details of processes (important though these are in real life, of course). The case examples are not intended to provide a complete simulation, and the focus is not on procedures but on how to work in a professional way. As you focus on the skills of self-management, communication, safeguarding and leadership, remember to think about how you would demonstrate professionalism, as discussed in Chapter 4. Keep thinking about the skills in the light of social work values, the use of power, critical analysis, supervision, emotional resilience, CPD and research mindedness.

In social work, there is rarely a single definitive or right answer, so we have not provided 'solutions'. The point of the extended examples is to give you the opportunity to use your professional skills to analyse and think critically about the scenarios at specified points in the story and to reflect on the implications for what it means to be a professional in social work today. We have suggested using models and ideas discussed in the earlier chapters, but these are not meant to be prescriptive. As with any case example, you will be working with limited information and may also feel that you would have approached some things differently. Your analysis will probably raise questions that cannot be answered. We encourage you to use these unanswered questions to deepen your thinking and perhaps stimulate discussion with your colleagues or do some further research of your own.

Case example 1: Working with adults

Part 1

You are a local authority social worker. The social services department has received a safeguarding alert regarding a man with learning disabilities from Andy Dacey, manager of St. Martin's day centre. At a recent review meeting for David Williams, aged 39, concerns were expressed by staff members that David's mother is giving away his money to a young woman who visits the house. It is said that this young woman has recently been dismissed from Premium, a private home care agency. Initial checking of records and other information establishes that there is reasonable cause to think that David meets the 'three key tests' that trigger the local authority's duty to make further safeguarding enquiries (Section 42 of the Care Act 2014):

- *he is an adult who has care and support needs (whether or not any of those needs are being met*);
- *he appears to be experiencing, or is at risk of, abuse or neglect (in this case, financial abuse)*; and
- *as a result of his care and support needs (related to his learning disability), it is reasonable to think that he may be unable to protect himself from the risk, or experience, of abuse or neglect.*

Your local authority has adopted the MSP approach (discussed in Chapter 7), and as the Enquiry Officer your first step is to arrange for a conversation to take place with David (or his representative) so that you can get a clearer idea about what is going on, whether there is a risk and, if so, what David wants to happen. Just as you are considering how best to approach David, the Duty Social Worker comes to tell you that she has just received a second safeguarding referral regarding Gwen Williams, aged 86 – who turns out to be David's mother. This referral is from Brenda Scott, the manager of Premium care agency, raising concerns about Gwen's self-neglect. You contact Brenda, who tells you that Gwen is currently unable to walk following a fall, and she is spending all day and night in her bed. Following a care assessment, she has twice-daily visits providing personal care and meals. Her condition has deteriorated over the past two weeks and the GP says that she urgently needs to be admitted to hospital. The problem is that Gwen refuses to go. To make matters worse, she is now refusing to let the care assistants into the house.

Reflection point 9.1

Before moving on, consider what you know at this point and what you still need to find out. You might find it helpful to look at the Anchor model's five questions, described in Chapter 7, even though there may not yet be enough information to answer them.

- *Using the Care Act 2014's three key tests (listed previously), is there a safeguarding duty in respect of Gwen?*

Part 2

Based on your initial information about Gwen, you may have judged that it is not clear whether there is a formal safeguarding duty. Gwen *does* have a need for care and support, and on the face of things it looks like her health and well-being may be at risk. At this point, however, you may feel that you lack the information to conclude that she is unable to protect herself. You discuss the situation with the Enquiry Manager (responsible for coordinating responses and decision-making, and ensuring that the local authority's safeguarding duty is discharged appropriately). You decide that, before talking with either David or Gwen, it would be a good idea to call an urgent meeting with the relevant agencies to share information, get a clearer picture and agree how best to approach the situation. At the meeting you take some notes for your own use, as follows:

Family:

- *Gwen Williams, aged 86 – White British, widow*
- *David Williams, aged 39 – White British, single*

Information from other professionals:

Andy Dacey (St. Martin's day centre) says that:

- *David has learning disabilities: he is physically fit but has partial hearing loss. He uses Makaton sign language to support his limited speech. David has been attending the day centre for about 14 years. Andy says David is reasonably self-sufficient in terms of personal care and can do simple household tasks such as washing up and using a kettle, toaster and microwave. He cannot read or manage money. Gwen, as his appointee, handles David's disability benefits. This is the money that, it is suggested, is being diverted to the young Polish woman. David has not been told of the allegation of financial abuse. Andy also shares the information that, at the review, David expressed a wish to move into the nearest town and live in his own flat or house. However, David is worried about leaving Gwen by herself.*

Dr Azim Khan (GP for both David and Gwen) reports that:

- *Gwen's mobility has been affected by arthritis for many years and she has a long-standing history of depression. Since her fall, she has been treated for dehydration, a chest infection, anaemia and pressure sores. She has now started to recover her strength, but Dr Khan would ideally like her to come into hospital for further assessment. Due to her physical frailty, if she does not receive adequate care and support at home, Gwen's health is likely to deteriorate again rapidly.*

Sally Doyle (District Nurse, lives locally) says that:

- *She has known the family since they arrived 20 years ago. Gwen used to run a riding school and she and David live in an isolated cottage, a mile from the village. Gwen's husband died of cancer many years ago. Despite long-standing health problems, she has managed without help until recently. Gwen and David live frugally. Gwen is a very 'private' person, and no one is sure whether she has any additional income to her state pension and carer's allowance. Sally says that the young Polish woman referred to by the day centre staff is Magda. Through her local knowledge, Sally is aware that Magda uses Gwen's bank card to purchase food, clothing and other items for herself and her young son. Gwen told Sally that Magda had full permission to use her bank card, but she did not seem to have a clear idea about the extent of the purchases.*

  A month ago, Gwen had a fall in the kitchen after David had gone to bed. She called for help, but David could not hear her. The next morning, he found Gwen on the kitchen floor but was unable to lift her. David has never learned how to use the phone because of his hearing loss, but fortunately the minibus arrived to collect him for the day centre and the driver called an ambulance. The paramedics assessed her and treated a minor cut on her head. They tried to persuade Gwen to come into hospital, but she shouted and swore at them and refused to go. Since then, Gwen says she cannot walk, instead apparently staying in her bed all day and night.

  Sally says that Gwen is getting very 'argumentative' and, when offered health advice or equipment, she insists that she doesn't need any help. Despite advice from Dr Khan and Sally, Gwen is apparently adamant that she will not go into hospital for any kind of treatment, even if a respite care place is found for David. She says that she does not need help from anyone except Magda, that David would be unhappy to go away and that when her time comes, she wants to 'die in her own bed'.

Brenda Scott (Premium care agency) reports that:

- *Due to her declining mobility in recent years, the agency has provided Gwen with two care assistant visits a week, supporting her with daily living and personal care tasks. As Gwen refuses to be financially assessed, she pays for these visits herself. Since her fall, Gwen has reluctantly agreed to pay for twice-daily care assistant visits 'until she is up and about again'. Over the past two weeks, Gwen has increasingly refused help and often sends the care assistants away as soon as they arrive. Later in the day, she phones the agency to complain about their behaviour. Gwen has become verbally abusive, making racist and other offensive comments about several care assistants, and Brenda is finding it hard to find anyone willing to work with her. With regard to Magda, Brenda says that she worked briefly for the care agency about six months previously, but was dismissed during her probationary period for failing to follow health and safety procedures. Brenda also reports that when care staff ask Gwen what shopping she wants or what she would like for tea, she often says, 'Magda will get it for me'. However, care staff sometimes arrive to find that Magda hasn't turned up after all – so there is no food in the house and Gwen has not eaten all day.*

At the meeting it is agreed that more information is needed before it can be decided whether David is at risk of financial abuse. You agree to have a conversation with Gwen to establish how David's money is being handled and to find out what financial arrangements Gwen has made with Magda. As for the risk to Gwen's health, the urgency that triggered the referral about her self-neglect has abated – but only temporarily. You will also review Gwen's care needs, liaising with Sally and Premium and establishing what support Magda is providing.

If Gwen is giving money away to Magda, the further question is raised whether she herself is at risk of financial abuse. There is much discussion in the meeting about whether Gwen's current behaviour indicates a decline in her mental health, or even dementia. Sally, however, says that Gwen has always been 'difficult' and 'argumentative'. Dr Khan agrees to refer her to the geriatrician for a specialist opinion. You agree to undertake a Mental Capacity Assessment to establish whether Gwen has the ability to decide on her care needs and to whom she gives her money.

It is also decided that you should explore David's wishes about where he wants to live (seen as pressing, in view of the uncertainty about Gwen's health and the possibility of hospital admission).

Reflection point 9.2

Consequent to the further information gained in the meeting, you should now be in a better position to start answering the Anchor model's five questions. Next, consider the following:

- *Your local authority has adopted the MSP process. As the allocated worker you need to 'have a conversation' with Gwen and get a clearer idea what is happening, whether there is a risk and, if there is, what she wants to happen. Who else would you talk with?*
- *What communication challenges might you encounter, and how would you address these? You may want to look back at Chapter 6 for ideas.*

Part 3

As Sally, the District Nurse, seems to have the best relationship with Gwen, you ask her to introduce you. When you arrive at the dilapidated cottage, Sally is talking with Magda who is folding clean laundry on the kitchen table. Magda says she must get off to pick her son up from school, and asks Sally to let Gwen know that she has cooked some food for David to reheat that evening.

Gwen is half propped-up in bed, looking very frail and dishevelled. She looks dismissively at you and mutters, 'another busy-body'. You attempt to establish rapport, but Gwen looks blankly at you until Sally realizes she doesn't have her hearing aids in. Several minutes elapse while the hearing aids are located, inserted and adjusted. You explain that because of the recent changes in Gwen's health, you need to review her care needs and make sure she is getting all possible help. At this stage, you do not mention that you are also beginning to gather information about Gwen's mental capacity. However, you do talk about the concerns regarding David's money and Magda's having access to her bank card; you also explain about the local authority's duty to make sure that David is safe. Gwen ignores all of this and starts to complain at length about the village shopkeepers. Sally takes her leave at this point. You attempt to bring Gwen back to the purpose of your visit. This is difficult because, despite her breathlessness and frequent coughing, Gwen talks continuously and in a complaining tone about various topics, including the inadequacies of Premium's care assistants, Dr Khan, Sally and the failings of the world in general.

Eventually, talking through Gwen's daily routine, you note that she appears to be very dependent on others for her meals, personal hygiene and medication. She tells you there is no need to worry about her: Magda looks after her 'like a daughter'. She speaks very fondly and admiringly of Magda and confirms that she gives her the bank card because she herself can't go out anywhere. She is aware that Magda sometimes uses this money to buy things for herself and her family, and regards this as a recompense for Magda's help. Gwen says she isn't concerned about the exact details of what Magda spends. As for David's money, after some rummaging in a carrier bag, Gwen hands you David's post office savings book and a recent account statement, from which you can see that David's benefit is regularly paid in, with no recent withdrawals. Gwen says that she gives David a few pounds spending money, from her own cash, when he goes to the day centre.

You have timed your visit hoping to meet David, and before long you hear the minibus. David comes upstairs and looks enquiringly at Gwen while making a sign that you recognize as a symbol for a cup of tea. She accepts and, while David goes down to the kitchen, Gwen comments that he can also heat up anything in the microwave if she explains the instructions. She tells you that David is 'like a child' but can look after himself, get dressed and 'keep himself clean'. When David returns with the tea, he starts tidying up around Gwen's bed, and you notice that he and Gwen communicate mainly by sign language, which seems to be a mixture of Makaton (of which you have some knowledge) and their own idiosyncratic signing. David then turns to you and speaks a few words, which you do not immediately catch. Gwen explains that he is inviting you to see his bedroom, and urges you to 'go and have a look'.

Across the corridor, David's room – although suffering from damp – is neat and tidy. He proudly points out his TV, neatly-arranged cupboards, and shelves displaying pictures and models of cars. As you acclimatize yourself to David's mixture of speech and gestures, you understand that he looks after his own room and likes it to be well-organized. Returning to Gwen, you find she has dozed off. You will have to return and continue your assessment on another day.

Reflection point 9.3

Pause to review what you have learned so far, using the Three Domains of Critical Practice reflective model described in Chapter 7. Remember that this model asks you to scrutinize any personal emotions and assumptions that you bring to the situation. You will also need to consider the situation from the standpoint of your professional knowledge; so, as well as your practice wisdom and knowledge of relevant laws and policies, think about the kinds of research evidence that you might draw on (or want to search for). The model also prompts you to consider the effects of structural disadvantage and power inequalities (again, you might need to research anything that is less familiar to you, such as the impact of rural communities on services).

Having completed this analysis, answer the following questions:

- *What is your evaluation – at this point – of the risks to David and Gwen?*
- *What further information do you need?*
- *How are you going to find out about David's wishes? (You may want to look at ideas in Chapter 6.)*
- *What personal emotions does this situation raise for you? Are there any personal or professional dilemmas? Thinking about the personal self-management skills discussed in Chapter 3, how might you manage these aspects of the case?*
- *Based on your analysis, can you see any potential opportunities to work in partnership with David and Gwen to achieve goals (reflect on the ideas in Chapter 5).*
- *Reviewing the ideas in Chapter 8, which leadership skills might enable you to make a positive difference in working with Gwen and David?*

Case example 2: Working with children and families

You respond to a referral from a headteacher that indicates that Jamie O'Brian, aged 12, might be at risk of harm due to unmet health and development needs. You make arrangements to carry out an initial assessment of Jamie's needs and the risk of significant harm.

Family:

- *Jamie O'Brian, aged 12 – White Irish*
- *Brigid Patel (mother), aged 31 – White Irish*
- *Ben Patel (step-father), aged 40 – South Asian*

Part 1

Before visiting the family, you check the case records. There is one previous referral from the primary school when Jamie was 8-years-old and had a cluster of bruises on both arms. After initial investigation, Mr Patel's explanation – that he had grabbed Jamie's arms to prevent him running into traffic – was considered consistent with the bruising. No other safeguarding concerns were identified and the case had been closed. The record from that time also notes from the School Nurse that Mr Patel was receiving a service from the Community Mental Health Team (CMHT) due to a diagnosis of anxiety and obsessive-compulsive disorder (OCD).

You contact the headteacher and hear that the current referral is due to mounting concerns about Jamie's arriving at school very hungry and in smelly, dirty clothes. He also has recurrent coughs and colds. Jamie has a statement of educational needs due to attention-deficit hyperactivity disorder (ADHD) and behavioural difficulties, and is supported by a classroom assistant. You establish that the difficult behaviour consists of Jamie shouting out inappropriately and throwing things (such as pencils and books) at other children during lessons, stealing sweets and food, and having temper tantrums. You are told that this behaviour has deteriorated in recent weeks. The educational psychologist reports that Jamie is emotionally and socially immature, and unusually 'clumsy'. He tends to be bullied by the other children. A dyslexia and dyspraxia assessment has been advised, but the school is awaiting the consent of Jamie's parents, who never come into school or reply to letters. The Headteacher comments that the father is very hostile towards anyone in authority, and staff who live locally say that that he has a drinking problem.

Reflection point 9.4

In preparing for the visit, what potential communication needs would you consider in relation to what you have heard about Jamie and his parents?

You may want to look at the ideas in Chapter 6 about building relationships with people who have had negative experiences of professional power. Whilst keeping an open mind, give some thought to how you could respond to potential resistance or hostility.

Part 2

You visit the family, who live in a small flat above a disused shop unit. The visit is conducted in a bedroom that is crowded with various items of furniture. It becomes clear that this is the flat's only habitable room, in which the whole family lives and sleeps. There is only one bed, and Jamie's parents point out a thin camping mattress rolled up in the corner, on which their son sleeps. Ben is unfriendly towards you, and during the visit he continually contradicts and interrupts Brigid. You detect alcohol on his breath. Jamie is said to be out playing.

It is obvious that the flat is in very poor repair, with strategically-placed buckets and other containers catching rain from the leaky roof. Apart from the bedroom, every room is filled with various bicycle parts, tools, cardboard boxes and bulging bin liners. Ben explains that these items are for his bike repair business. You observe that the flat is not very clean, and littered with used crockery and scraps of food. There is no working bathroom and the toilet is broken. The small kitchen is sparsely equipped, and the sink appears to double as a washbasin. The family seems to be struggling financially. Ben says his self-employment brings in enough money (but from Brigid's expression you think this may not be quite true). Brigid has two part-time jobs, working as an office cleaner in the early mornings and doing various shifts in a supermarket.

Brigid expresses concern that Jamie is 'acting up' at school, but seems at a loss to suggest any reasons for this. She says that Jamie is a good boy and helps his dad when Brigid is on the evening shift. At this point, Jamie arrives and sits quietly on a chair in the hall, eating a packet of crisps. Ben is loudly critical of Jamie, telling you he is 'stupid', 'weak' and 'disobedient'. You start to talk to Jamie, but at this point Ben gets angry and tells you to leave 'before [he] makes [you]'.

Reflection point 9.5

Use the Anchor model's five questions, described in Chapter 7, as a guide to consider what you know at this point.

- *What else do you need to find out and how might you obtain this information?*

Part 3

The next day, Brigid appears at your office and anxiously apologizes that Ben had been 'having a bad day'. She knows the flat is a mess but assures you that they will have it cleaned up and get repairs done as soon as they can afford it. She explains that Ben is 'not very well' at present and he suffers from painful arthritis in his hips. Brigid says that Ben used to sell bikes and do repairs from the shop below the flat, but he went out of business when he became too ill to work. Of Jamie's coughs and colds, she says he has always suffered from them and does not seem to make any connection with their damp living conditions.

Brigid goes on to tell you something of the family history. She grew up in the Republic of Ireland, and was 19 and unmarried when Jamie was born. She did not remain in touch with his father. Brigid left Jamie with her maternal grandparents while she came to England to 'start afresh', visiting Jamie once a year. While working in a hotel, Brigid met and later married Ben, who had grown up in care. She moved into the flat and shop, which Ben had inherited from a childless uncle. Five years ago, Brigid's parents died within months of each other. Jamie stayed with Brigid's (married) sister for a few months and then came to England to live with Brigid and Ben.

You visit Jamie in school. He is a friendly and gently-spoken boy (despite the reports about his tantrums), but you sense that he is a little guarded and seems worried that you will 'send [him] away'. He appears very embarrassed when you refer to the living conditions in the flat. He speaks appreciatively of the teaching assistant, who lets him use the staff shower and gives him clean clothes and breakfast. Jamie does not say much about his parents, and you notice that he refers to them as 'Brigid and Ben'.

You make a further visit to the family home to gain Ben's perspective, but despite your best efforts he remains resistant and hostile. He clams up entirely when you ask about his health and whether he still receives a service from the CMHT. Brigid begins to answer for him and he tells her to 'shut up talking'. He then turns to you and says he hates all social workers because they 'were useless' when he was in care. Sounding emotional, he says Brigid is his only family and the one person who has ever cared for him. He refuses to discuss anything else and insists you leave.

Following this visit, you contact the CMHT, who confirm that Ben is no longer receiving a service. The GP informs you that Ben has a repeat prescription for medication to treat his anxiety, and neither he nor any other members of the family have attended the surgery over the past 18 months.

Reflection point 9.6

Now that you have a little more information, using the Three Domains of Critical Practice try and make sense of what you have learned about the family. Remember to consider each area, as you did for the first case example. Then answer the following questions:

- *What are your personal emotions and views about this situation?*
- *In trying to understand what may be happening for Jamie, Brigid and Ben, what does your professional knowledge and practice wisdom tell you, and what other research evidence would you like to have?*
- *How might structural disadvantage and power inequalities be impacting, and to what extent could your practice be sensitive to, or help to address, this?*
- *Your focus is on Jamie's safety and well-being. How might this influence your practice, and how would you respond to his parents' needs and perspectives?*

Part 4

You complete your initial assessment and, because of multiple risk factors, you conclude that Jamie's physical and emotional needs are not being adequately met. After a strategy discussion and an Initial Child Protection Conference (section 47, Children Act 1989), a Child Protection Plan is put in place. Brigid – and Ben, with reluctance – agree to make a number of changes that will provide a more healthful physical and emotional environment for Jamie, which include making repairs that will resolve some of the damp and clearing space to enable Jamie to have his own bedroom, be able to look after his personal hygiene and have clean clothes for school. The family is offered practical support to help achieve this. As part of the plan, you will attempt to work with the whole family, as well as visiting Jamie weekly at school. The plan is to be reviewed in three months.

Reflection point 9.7

- *Would you include anything else in the Child Protection Plan and, if so, what would you include, and why?*
- *What would your aims be for working with Jamie, and how would you use one of the communication methods described in Chapter 6?*
- *What would your aims be for working with the family, and how would you go about this?*
- *Looking back at Chapter 5 in the light of your analysis so far, how would you determine the potential for supporting Jamie's parents to 'self-manage' the changes that are needed?*
- *How would you use leadership skills (discussed in Chapter 8) to support your work with the family and other professionals?*

Now imagine that your agency is using the *SoS* approach, and look at the example of an Assessment and Planning Form in Chapter 7 (see Figure 7.1).

- *What would you hope to see written on this document given your work with Jamie and his family?*

Part 5

With practical help offered by a Family Support Worker, some progress is made within the home. Ben's GP refers him for physiotherapy to manage the effects of his arthritis. After a few weeks, progress comes to a halt, and as the review date draws near, the bathroom has not been repaired and Jamie still has no bedroom or bed. The school remains concerned about Jamie's health and behaviour, neither of which have improved. Your attempts to work with the whole family have had limited success, as one or both parents tend not to be at home for pre-arranged appointments.

Jamie does, however, respond quite well to your regular sessions in school, and you begin to establish trust and gain a clearer picture of his day-to-day life. You find that many tensions and uncertainties are evident in his relationship with his parents. It emerges that he initially grew up believing that his grandparents were his parents and, even now, he sometimes seems doubtful about whether Brigid really is his mother. Some days, Jamie appears preoccupied and anxious, and in one of your sessions he cries inconsolably. Recently, you have noticed scratches on his arms, which Jamie eventually admits he did to himself.

Failing to gain entry on your home visits, you invite both parents to the office so that you can discuss this worrying development, but they do not answer your letters or phone calls.

One Monday morning you receive a phone call from the Headteacher to say that Jamie has arrived very dirty and with bad bruises. You immediately go to the school and find Jamie eating breakfast in the staff room: staff say he was 'ravenous'. The bruises cover both hands. Jamie tells you that on Saturday, Ben had 'gone berserk' and attacked him with a saucepan. He appears to have protected his head with his hands, but shows you other bruises on his legs and back. Jamie says that Ben prevented him from leaving the flat, though early this morning he had managed to get out while his parents were asleep. He discloses other occasions over the past year when Ben had hit him and says that he is too scared to go home.

You consult your manager, who applies for an Emergency Protection Order (EPO). This is granted, and a medical examination confirms that Jamie's story is consistent with his injuries. A short-term foster placement is obtained for the same day. You prepare to visit Brigid and Ben.

Reflection point 9.8

Given this further information, update the Anchor model's five questions. Then, answer the following questions:

- *At this point, what might be going through your mind? For example, do you feel confident, anxious, upset, etc.? Thinking about your own emotional resilience, what will you do with these feelings? Who would you talk with? You might want to look back at Chapter 3 for suggestions about managing difficult personal emotions.*
- *As this situation unfolds, what issues will you consider for your own and others' physical safety?*

Part 6

Following investigation and further assessment, your agency commences care proceedings, starting with an Interim Care Order. Jamie settles well with the foster parents, and his health and behaviour at school are improving.

Despite concerted attempts to meet with Brigid and Ben, they do not respond. Brigid is offered supervised contact visits, but does not take these up. She does, however, send texts to Jamie, and on one occasion they meet without telling you or the foster parents. According to Jamie, Brigid plans to leave Ben and make a home for Jamie. Jamie seems excited about this. Suddenly, Brigid's texts stop. When you call to see Ben, he opens the door and tells you, tearfully, that Brigid has left him and returned to Ireland. Brigid writes to Jamie saying that she will send for him as soon as she gets settled.

Reflection point 9.9

At this point, you will want to reflect on what this new information means. For the purpose of the case example, think about whether or not this changes the picture that you have built up. Again, reflect on any personal emotions and personal or professional dilemmas: how might you manage these?

Finally, we suggest that you create a decision tree, described in Chapter 7, to weigh up all the possible recommendations that you might make at this point. Remember that a decision tree does *not* replace your professional judgement, but it can be a helpful conceptual tool to aid your thinking. It can prompt you to explore different possibilities and to articulate the rationale for recommending one option over another. It can also promote thinking about how a potential course of action could be made more successful.

Summary and conclusion

We hope that these two in-depth case examples have enabled you to practise using the tools, models and ideas discussed earlier in the book. We also hope that the inevitable shortcomings and limitations in these fictional scenarios will stimulate you to carry on asking questions, and to look for answers in your CPD, discussions with your colleagues and your own critical reflection. Keep on challenging yourself and your colleagues to ask, 'Where is the professionalism?' and 'How is professionalism impacting on this task?' as you go about everyday social work activities.

Key points from this chapter

- A key skill for professionalism is to critically analyse and review all sources of information, including your own personal response to service users' lives and experiences, at each stage of social work intervention.
- In-depth analysis, taking account of structural disadvantage and inequalities, is likely to highlight differing perspectives and this may raise dilemmas and conflicts.
- Self-awareness – gained through critical analysis and professional supervision – regarding your personal response to service users' experiences, and to personal and professional dilemmas, is an important aspect of maintaining emotional resilience.
- Skills of professional leadership and self-management are essential elements of working constructively with complexity and risk.
- Critical analysis will help you to consider the most empowering ways of communicating and working in partnership with service users.

10 Conclusion

In this chapter, we revisit some key themes and debates and extend these to address the ethical implications for practising professionalism (and self-management) skills.

We have argued, in **Chapters 1** and **2**, that, conceptually, professionalism is contested and, in social work, it is not universally accepted that professionalization is a 'good thing'. As we showed in those chapters, a certain conception or standard of professionalism in social work has been enforced from the outside by governments, ostensibly keen to increase the skill base and knowledge of the workforce. Achieving this has led to increased oversight of social workers through inspections of services, and instigation of detailed procedures about what professionals should do in given situations. Taking England as an illustration, even regarding CPD, there are guidelines about how much training social workers should undertake within a given period, and this is taken into account in their (re)registration (HCPC 2017). Thus, a possible downside to the professionalization of social work is a reduction in professionals' autonomy and decision-making about their work. This has been termed 'de-professionalization' (Thompson 2016).

It is a paradoxical situation that, as governments attempt to increase the professional status of social work – and as professionals acquire more power (in law) to intervene in people's lives to protect them and enhance their well-being – social workers also have less discretion and autonomy in practice (although, see Evans [2012], who argues that this apparent loss of autonomy is overstated and that practitioners exercise discretion in 'rule-saturated organizations'). Opponents of professionalization point to the proliferation of procedures, guidance and processes as examples of the reduced autonomy of social workers in the era of professionalism. This latter point also applies to professionals' scope to self-manage their careers, including their learning and development. Returning to the earlier point about CPD, the need to follow externally-imposed training targets could also mean a diminishing scope to follow the model implied in Exercise 3.1. This is because formal employer training programmes may have less scope for reflection and reflexivity, and may be designed to teach professionals about organizational processes (Gould and Baldwin 2004). Even regarding skills to assist other people to self-manage (Chapter 5), teaching programmes could be used as a rationale for rationing because, if people can be taught to manage their own affairs, the state can forego its duty to provide them with services.

Notwithstanding this, as we explained in Chapter 2, our formulation of professionalism is based on the shared norms and culture of the social work professional group. Our aim in this book therefore has been to explore the skills that are considered indispensable to effective practice. For example, within social work, it is not controversial to argue that the skills discussed – self-management, communication, safeguarding and risk management, and leadership – as well as skills for supporting others to self-manage are essential to 'good' practice. Given this consensus, we have aimed to outline *how* professionals can attain and enhance these skills through case examples and exercises.

In **Chapter 3** we contextualized the overall message of the book by highlighting some psychological factors required for professionalism. We discussed self-motivation to maintain the highest practice and ethical standards. Situated within practice, motivation is important because it enables practitioners to attempt *prima facie* difficult tasks and, when successful, it can form the basis for increased self-efficacy. From this vantage point, in **Chapter 4** we outlined the key elements essential for successful professionalism. One example here is 'self-awareness about professional and personal values'. In order to be professional, one must have the capacity to reflect on the conduct and behaviour consistent with the title 'social worker'. Self-awareness and reflection also feature strongly in our exploration of professional communication skills in **Chapter 6**. We argued that apart from being skilful in the general art of communicating, the ability to reflect on how professional power shapes interaction with service users is another critical capability for social workers. The power inherent in the title 'social worker' can affect the words used to describe people and/or their situations, the tone adopted by professionals, and how social workers communicate with service users. In this communicative regard, a social worker's oratory skills would be unethical if deployed to misrepresent service users' needs. Similarly, effective communication skills can be put to unethical use by persuading service users to 'consent' to plans that the professional knows are not in their best interests. Thus, our call for skilful and increased professionalism is also an advocacy for these to be symbiotic with developed moral character (Clark 2006) in social workers: social workers should enhance their professional skills *in tandem with* developing good moral character.

Keeping to ethics, in **Chapter 7** we explored the professional skills required to successfully safeguard service users who have been harmed or are at risk of harm. We noted the complexity of the term 'safeguarding' and its different professional interpretations. Echoing the previous expositions in Chapter 3 on self-management, we showed in Chapter 7 the complexity of emotions, value judgements and professional skills that combine to determine safeguarding assessments. Here, too, there are fine ethical decisions to make because, in order to protect people, social workers may have to curtail their rights. In other instances, assessments about whether people are at risk can be affected by their socio-economic position. In this respect, the Three Domains of Critical Practice: Reflective Tool (Figure 7.3) can assist readers to identify their value-base, enabling them to understand how this shapes their assessments about the risks faced by service users.

In **Chapter 8** we discussed leadership, which has profound ethical implications for social work because it is tied to exercising power. Here, we showed that practitioners perform leadership roles in all aspects of their work, and that some models are more ethically desirable than others. On our part, we support a servant leadership model because of the stress on equality between 'leader' and 'follower'.

The model also accords to the principles of self-determination in social work and reflects the motivating rationale for most people who train as social workers. In our discussion of servant leadership, we discussed the skills required for adopting it in practice. We hope that we successfully debunked the supposition that leadership implies the acquisition of formal titles or roles. We hope, also, that we showed how professionals exercise some aspects of leadership in their routine practice. In the closing stages of this book we return to **Chapter 5**, which was about self-management, maintaining the ongoing thematic focus on ethics.

Reflecting on the ethics of self-management

The essence of self-management is that people draw on internal resources to resolve their difficulties and/or control problematic aspects of their lives. Contextualized within professionalism, this means that professionals assume primary responsibility for shaping their careers through training. It also implies mastery over the psychological aspects of our role such as dealing with stress and emotional labour, and drawing on self-motivation and self-efficacy. The role of professionals also extends to enabling service users to develop skills to self-manage, to remove the necessity for state intervention in their lives. In the rest of this chapter, we discuss some ethical implications of enabling service users' self-management.

One consequence is *ethical trespass*. This concept, adopted by Weinberg (2005) from the work of Mellissa Ollie, refers to 'the harm that follows from one's actions, sometimes unintended or unforeseen, because in action some options are opened, whereas others are foreclosed' (Weinberg 2005: 331). The concept suggests that in our everyday practice, our decisions can unintentionally result in harm to others. As professionals, we're involved in a statutory system for distributing resources and implementing laws, rules and regulations. Due to the legal duties associated with our professional titles, we do not have autonomy to decide otherwise. For instance, in children's services in England, social workers have a legal duty to conduct investigations into reports of harm or probable risk to children (HM Government 2015). The concept of ethical trespass postulates that in performing this assessment duty, social workers' actions may lead to others being harmed, even despite their intentions. We provide a practice example here to illustrate ethical trespass in self-management.

Practice example 10.1

Mr Alexander is 80-years-old and has a long-term heart condition. Mr Alexander lives with his wife and was hospitalized after an acute phase of his illness. While recovering, medical staff informed Mr Alexander that they were reluctant to discharge him without home support. However, keen to maintain his independence, Mr Alexander refused domiciliary support. In keeping with the social work values of self-determination and empowerment, the hospital social worker, Tanya, enlisted Mr Alexander on the hospital's self-management programme. Mr Alexander was discharged after satisfying staff that he could oversee his care needs at home. Two days later, while getting out of the bath, Mr Alexander slipped, fell and broke his leg.

Reflection point 10.1

- *What are the emotions that the social worker will feel?*
- *What are your views about the social worker's actions?*
- *Can you debate the ethical standpoints of the medical team and the social worker?*
- *Should the medical team have simply discharged Mr Alexander when he first told them that he did not want support services?*

In Practice Example 10.1, Tanya respected Mr Alexander's wishes for and right to self-determination, and enlisted him on a self-management programme for him to learn to oversee his care. However, the unintended consequence of this action was that, without assistance at home, Mr Alexander slipped. Tanya may have felt guilt, self-recrimination and may even have lost confidence in her judgement. Her managers may have held her accountable for her decision. However, arguably Tanya made the right decision, ethically, to respect Mr Alexander's wishes. Weinberg (2005) argues that the concept of ethical trespass enables us to accept and process the fact that some of our decisions may unwittingly lead to harm or the wrong outcomes for people. This is important in self-management: in seeking to support people to manage their care (see Chapter 5), service users may be exposed to some risk, but this is balanced against the need to enhance their autonomy. On the other hand, we may be requested by our managers to leave people to manage on their own without services as part of self-management. This presents ethical challenges, which we discuss next.

Taylor (2007) used the term 'professional dissonance' to refer to the 'discomfort' that professionals feel when they are forced to implement policies or take actions conflicting with their personal values. We use a practice example to illustrate this.

In Practice Example 10.2, professional dissonance arises because Jo believes that the children's 'neglect' has been caused by lack of access to services and money. She believes that if the family had adequate income, Sarah would be able to heat the house and buy food for the children. Jo also believes that poverty may have caused Sarah to develop low mood, hence the desire to remain in bed instead of playing with her children. Jo is working from an *anti-oppressive* stance

Reflection point 10.2

As a newly-qualified social worker, Jo is tasked with assessing the needs of the Brown siblings, who reported to school in dirty clothes. On receiving the referral, Jo read the case records and learnt that the children are regularly referred to children's services and were subject to Child Protection Plans (CPPs) two years ago. When Jo visited the home, she observed that there was little food in the fridge and the house was very cold. Additionally, the children's mother, Sarah, remained in bed throughout the afternoon when they returned from school, instead of feeding and playing with them. Jo's view was that the family were victims of poverty (for more on child poverty, see Bywaters 2013; Bywaters et al. 2016) and, to mitigate this, the family should be provided with a regular income by children's services. Jo's manager, Alexa, instead directs her to work towards developing another CPP and a referral to parenting classes. Her reasoning is that Sarah needs to 'learn' about the benefits of playing with her children and exercising for her mental health; this will enable her to manage her home and mental health better.

because she believes that structural inequality explains the family's situation. However, her manager takes a different view, believing that Sarah bears some responsibility for the children's condition. Based on the theorization by Taylor (2007), Jo's professional dissonance would be caused by her implementing her manager's direction that conflicts with her own values. We can also see here that self-management has been deployed by the team manager to deny vital services to the family.

Exercise 10.1: Recalling experiences of ethical stress and professional dissonance

Referring to the work of Weinberg (2005) and Taylor (2007):

- Recall a time your actions may have caused harm to other people unintentionally or inadvertently.
- Discuss with a colleague or friend an occasion when you were required to follow directions that conflicted with your values.
- Discuss your feelings and how you managed your conflicting emotions.

As a final note, we want to acknowledge the difficult employment conditions of social workers (at least in England), which arguably impede professionalism and self-management. Most social workers have high caseloads, less time to engage directly with service users and reduced training budgets. In this context, it can be argued that organizations are foregoing their duty to provide the necessary structures to support professional practice. However, arguably the current situation reinforces the need for us, as social workers, to maintain our shared values and draw on the skills that we all agree are essential to providing good outcomes for users of our services. These are the skills outlined in this book, which we hope practitioners will find useful in their admirable work.

References

Akhtar, F. (2013) *Mastering Social Work Values and Ethics*. London: Jessica Kingsley.

Alaszewski, A. and Alaszewski, H. (2002) Towards the creative management of risk: perceptions, practices and policies, *British Journal of Learning Disabilities*, 30 (2): 56–62.

Alvesson, M. and Spicer, A. (2012) Critical leadership studies: the case for critical performativity, *Human Relations*, 65 (3): 367–390.

Avolio, B.J., Walumbwa, F.O. and Weber, T.J. (2009) Leadership: current theories, research, and future directions, *Annual Review of Psychology*, 60: 421–449.

Baginsky, M., Moriarty, J., Manthorpe, J. et al. (2017) *Evaluation of Signs of Safety in 10 pilots*, Research Report DFE-RR589. London: Department for Education. Available at: https://www.gov.uk/government/publications/signs-of-safety-practice-in-childrens-services-an-evaluation (accessed 31 August 2017).

Baker, R., Angus, D., Smith-Conway, E. et al. (2015) Visualising conversations between care home staff and residents with dementia, *Ageing and Society*, 35 (2): 270–297.

Bandura, A. (1994) *Self-efficacy*. Available at: https://www.uky.edu/~eushe2/Bandura/BanEncy.html (accessed 5 January 2018).

Banks, S. (2012) *Ethics and Values in Social Work*. Basingstoke: Palgrave Macmillan.

Barclay, P. Sir (1982) *Social Workers: Their Role and Tasks*. London: Bedford Square Press.

Barlow, J., Fisher, J.D. and Jones, D. (2012) *Systematic review of models of analysing significant harm*, Research Report DFE-RR199. London: Department for Education. Available at: https://www.gov.uk/government/publications/systematic-review-of-models-of-analysing-significant-harm (accessed 3 September 2017).

Barnes, D., Carpenter, J. and Dickinson, C. (2000) Interprofessional education for community mental health: attitudes to community care and professional stereotypes, *Social Work Education*, 19 (6): 565–583.

Barnett, R. (1997) *Higher Education: A Critical Business*. Buckingham: SRHE and Open University Press.

Barry, M. (2007) *Effective Approaches to Risk Assessment in Social Work: An International Literature Review: Final Report*. Edinburgh: Scottish Executive Social Research. Available at: http://www.gov.scot/Resource/Doc/194419/0052192.pdf. (accessed 26 July 2018).

Beddoe, L., Davys, A. and Adamson, C. (2013) Educating resilient practitioners, *Social Work Education*, 32 (1): 100–117.

Bennett, N., Wise, C., Woods, P. et al. (2003) *Distributed leadership: A review of literature*. Nottingham: National College for School Leadership. Available at: http://oro.open.ac.uk/8534/1/bennett-distributed-leadership-full.pdf (accessed 11 May 2018).

Biggs, J. and Tang, C. (2007) *Teaching for Quality Learning at University*, 4th edn. Buckingham: SHRE and Open University Press.

Blok, A.C. (2017) A middle-range explanatory theory of self-management behavior for collaborative research and practice, *Nursing Forum*, 52 (2): 138–146.

Bodenheimer, T., Lorig K., Holman, H. et al. (2002) Patient self-management of chronic disease in primary care, *Journal of the American Medical Association*, 288 (19): 2469–2475.

Boehm, A. and Yoels, N. (2009) Effectiveness of welfare organizations: the contribution of leadership styles, staff cohesion, and worker empowerment, *British Journal of Social Work*, 39 (7): 1360–1380.

Bogo, M., Regehr, C., Baird, S. et al. (2017) Cognitive and affective elements of practice confidence in social work students and practitioners, *British Journal of Social Work*, 47 (3): 701–718.

Bolden, R. (2011) Distributed leadership in organizations: a review of theory and research, *International Journal of Management Reviews*, 13 (3): 251–269.

Bosk, E.A., Van Alst, D. and Scoyoc, V.A. (2017) A chronic problem: competing paradigms for substance abuse in child welfare policy and practice and the need for new approaches, *British Journal of Social Work*, 47 (6): 1669–1685.

Brandon, M., Glaser, D., Maguire, S. et al. (2014) *Missed opportunities: Indicators of neglect – what is ignored, why, and what can be done?* Research Report DFE-RR404. London: Department for Education. Available at: http://www.cwrc.ac.uk/documents/RR404_-_Indicators_of_neglect_missed_opportunities.pdf (accessed 17 September 2017).

British Association of Social Workers (BASW) (2012a) *Continuing professional development (CPD) policy*. Birmingham: BASW. Available at: http://cdn.basw.co.uk/upload/basw_120605-9.pdf (accessed 25 October 2017).

British Association of Social Workers (BASW) (2012b) *Professional Capabilities Framework: Social work level capabilities*. Birmingham: BASW. Available at: https://www.basw.co.uk/pcf/PCF05SocialWorkLevelCapabilities.pdf (accessed 14 May 2018).

British Association of Social Workers (BASW) (2014) *Code of ethics for social work*. Birmingham: BASW. Available at: www.basw.co.uk/codeofethics/ (accessed 3 April 2018).

British Association of Social Workers (BASW) (n.d.) *Professional capability framework – social work level capabilities*. Birmingham: BASW. Available at: https://www.basw.co.uk/pcf/PCF05SocialWorkLevelCapabilities.pdf (accessed 20 November 2017).

British Deaf Association (BDA) (2018) *What we stand for*. London: BDA. Available at: https://bda.org.uk/history/what-we-stand-for/ (accessed 25 March 2018).

Broadhurst, K., Shaw, M., Kershaw, S. et al. (2015) Vulnerable birth mothers and repeat losses of infants to public care: is targeted reproductive health care ethically defensible?, *Journal of Social Welfare and Family Law*, 37 (1): 84–98.

Broadhurst, K., Wastell, D., White, S. et al. (2010) Performing 'initial assessment': Identifying the latent conditions for error at the front-door of local authority children's services, *British Journal of Social Work*, 40 (2): 352–370.

Brown, L., Moore, S. and Turney, D. (2012) *Analysis and Critical Thinking in Assessment*. Dartington: Research in Practice.

Buchanan, I. (2011) Policy swings and roundabouts: social work in shifting social and economic contexts, in J. Seden, S. Matthews, M. McCormick and A. Morgan (eds.) *Professional Development in Social Work*. Abingdon: Routledge.

Bunn, A. (2013) *Signs of Safety in England: An NSPCC commissioned report on the Signs of Safety model in child protection*. London: NSPCC. Available at: https://www.nspcc.org.uk/services-and-resources/research-and-resources/2013/signs-of-safety-model-england/ (accessed 22 August 2017).

Bywaters, P. (2013) Inequalities in child welfare: towards a new policy, research and action agenda, *British Journal of Social Work*, 45 (1): 6–23.

Bywaters, P., Bunting, L., Davidson, G. et al. (2016) *The relationship between poverty, child abuse and neglect: An evidence review*. York: Joseph Rowntree Foundation. Available at: https://www.jrf.org.uk/report/relationship-between-poverty-child-abuse-and-neglect-evidence-review (accessed 31 May 2018).

Care UK (2015) *Listen, talk, connect. Communicating with people living with dementia: a guide for carers, relatives and friends*. Colchester: Care UK. Available at: http://www.careuk.com/sites/rcs/files/Care_UK_rcs_LTC.pdf (accessed 4 January 2018).

Carpenter, J., Shardlow, S.M., Patsios, D. et al. (2015) Developing the confidence and competence of newly qualified child and family social workers in England: outcomes of a national programme, *British Journal of Social Work*, 45 (1): 153–176.

Carr, S. (2010) *Enabling risk, ensuring safety: Self-directed support and personal budgets*, SCIE Report 36. London: SCIE. Available at: http://www.scie.org.uk/publications/reports/report36/ (accessed 22 August 2017).

Clark, C. (2006) Moral character in social work, *British Journal of Social Work*, 36 (1): 75–89.

Cole, A. (2012) Direct payment fraud: a tragic case of murder and neglect, *The Guardian*, 18 January. Available at: https://www.theguardian.com/society/2012/jan/18/direct-payment-fraud-murder-neglect (accessed 30 August 2017).

Collins, S. (2007) Social workers, resilience, positive emotions and optimism, *Practice*, 19 (4): 255–269.

Collins, S. (2008) Statutory social workers: stress, job satisfaction, coping, social support and individual differences, *British Journal of Social Work*, 38(6): 1173–1193.

Community Care (2012) Four in ten social workers say homophobia is 'problem in the profession', *Community Care*, 31 July. Available at: http://www.communitycare.co.uk/2012/07/31/four-in-ten-social-workers-say-homophobia-is-problem-in-the-profession/ (accessed 20 August 2017).

Cooper, B. (2008) Continuing professional development: a critical approach, in A.W. Fraser and S. Matthews (eds.) *The Critical Practitioner in Social Work and Health Care*. London: Sage.

Cooper, B., Gordon, J. and Rixon, A. (2015) *Best Practice with Children and Families: Critical Social Work Stories*. Basingstoke: Palgrave Macmillan.

Corben, S. and Rosen, R. (2005) *Self-management for long-term conditions: Patients' perspectives on the way ahead*, Working Paper. London: King's Fund. Available at: https://www.kingsfund.org.uk/sites/files/kf/field/field_publication_file/self-management-long-term-conditions-patients-perspectives-sara-corben-rebecca-rosen-kings-fund-26-july-2005.pdf (accessed 17 January 2017).

Cowburn, M. (2000) Consultancy to groupwork programmes for adult male sex offenders: some reflections on knowledge and processes, *British Journal of Social Work*, 5 (1): 635–664.

Croisdale-Appleby, D. (2014) *Re-visioning social work education: An independent review*. Available at: https://www.gov.uk/government/publications/social-work-education-review (accessed 16 August 2016).

Cullen, A.F. (2013) 'Leaders in our own lives': suggested indications for social work leadership from a study of social work practice in a palliative care setting, *British Journal of Social Work*, 43 (8): 1527–1544.

Daily Telegraph (2010) Student guilty of killing 'controlling' father and burying him in concrete, *Daily Telegraph*, 8 September. Available at: http://www.telegraph.co.uk/news/uknews/crime/7990744/Student-guilty-of-killing-controlling-father-and-burying-him-in-concrete.html (accessed 21 August 2017).

Dalzell, R. and Sawyer, E. (2011) *Putting Analysis into Assessment: Undertaking Assessments of Need – A Toolkit for Practitioners*, 2nd rev. edn. London: National Children's Bureau.

Dathan, M. (2013) Does your accent really hinder your job prospects?, *The Guardian*, 22 November. Available at: https://www.theguardian.com/careers/accent-hinder-job-prospects (accessed 25 March 2018).

D'Cruz, H., Gillingham, P. and Melendez, S. (2007) Reflexivity, its meanings and relevance to social work: a critical review of the literature, *British Journal of Social Work*, 37 (1): 73–90.

Dementia UK (2017) *Life story work*. London: Dementia UK. Available at: https://www.dementiauk.org/for-professionals/free-resources/life-story-work/ (accessed 4 January 2018).

Department for Constitutional Affairs (2005) *The Mental Capacity Act 2005*. London: The Stationery Office.

Department for Constitutional Affairs (2007) *The Mental Capacity Act: Code of Practice*. London: The Stationery Office.

Department for Education (2015) *Knowledge and skills statements for child and family social work*. Available at: https://www.gov.uk/government/publications/knowledge-and-skills-statements-for-child-and-family-social-work (accessed 20 August 2017).

Department of Health (2015) *Knowledge and skills statement for social workers in adult services*. Available at: https://www.gov.uk/government/uploads/system/uploads/attachment_data/file/411957/KSS.pdf (accessed 20 August 2017).

Department of Health (2016) *Care and support statutory guidance*. Available at: https://www.gov.uk/government/publications/care-act-statutory-guidance/care-and-support-statutory-guidance (accessed 18 December 2017).

de Silva, D. (2011) *Helping people help themselves: A review of the evidence considering whether it is worthwhile to support self-management*. London: The Health Foundation. Available at: http://www.health.org.uk/sites/health/files/HelpingPeopleHelpThemselves.pdf (accessed 18 November 2017).

DeWalt, D.A., Davis, T.C., Wallace, A.S. et al. (2009) Goal setting in diabetes self-management: taking the baby steps to success, *Patient Education and Counseling*, 77 (2): 218–223.

Doel, M., Allmark, P.J., Conway, P. et al. (2009) Professional boundaries: crossing a line or entering the shadows?, *British Journal of Social Work*, 40 (6): 1866–1889.

Duffy, F. (2017) A social work perspective on how ageist language, discourses and understandings negatively frame older people and why taking a critical social work stance is essential, *British Journal of Social Work*, 47 (7): 2068–2085.

Dumbrill, G.C. (2006) Parental experience of child protection services: a qualitative study, *Child Abuse and Neglect*, 30 (1): 27–37.

Dunning, J. (2011) Social workers failed to monitor elderly man murdered by son, *Community Care*, 7 November. Available at: http://www.communitycare.co.uk/2011/11/07/social-workers-failed-to-monitor-elderly-man-murdered-by-son/ (accessed 22 August 2017).

Eccles, J.S. and Wigfield, A. (2002) Motivational beliefs, values, and goals, *Annual Review of Psychology*, 53: 109–132.

Evans, L. (2008) *Professionalism, professionality and the development of education professionals*. Available at: http://eprints.whiterose.ac.uk/4077/2/Professionalism_professionality_and_the_development_of_educational_professionals_version_submitted_to_BJES.pdf (accessed 28 May 2018).

Evans, T. (2012) Organisational rules and discretion in adult social work, *British Journal of Social Work*, 43 (4): 1–20.

Evetts, J. (2003) The sociological analysis of professionalism: occupational change in the modern world, *International Sociology*, 18 (2): 395–415.

Evetts, J. (2006) The sociology of professional groups: new directions, *Current Sociology*, 54 (1): 133–143.

Evetts, J. (2012) Professionalism: value and ideology, *Sociopedia.isa*. Available at: http://www.sagepub.net/isa/resources/pdf/Professionalism.pdf (accessed 14 May 14 2018).

Evetts, J. (2014) The concept of professionalism: professional work, professional practice and learning, in S. Billett, C. Harteis and H. Gruber (eds.) *International Handbook of Research in Professional and Practice-based Learning*. Dordrecht: Springer.

Fairtlough, A. (2017) *Professional Leadership for Social Work Practitioners and Educators*. Abingdon: Routledge.

Ferguson, H. (2011) *Child Protection Practice*. Basingstoke: Palgrave Macmillan.

Fields, J.W., Thompson, K.C. and Hawkins, J.R. (2015) Servant leadership: teaching the helping professional, *Journal of Leadership Education*, 14 (4): 92–105.

Fook, J. (2015) Reflective practice and critical reflection, in J. Lishman (ed.) *Handbook for Practice Learning in Social Work and Social Care: Knowledge and Theory*, 3rd edn. London: Jessica Kingsley.

Fook, J. and Askeland, G.A. (2006) Challenges of critical reflection: nothing ventured, nothing gained, *Social Work Education*, 16 (2): 1–14.

Fook, J., Ryan, M. and Hawkins, L. (2000) *Professional Expertise: Practice, Theory and Education for Working in Uncertainty*. London: Whiting & Birch.

Forrester, D. and Harwin, J. (2006) Parental substance misuse and child care social work: findings from the first stage of a study of 100 families, *Child and Family Social Work*, 11 (4): 325–335.

Forrester, D., McCambridge, J., Waissbein, C. et al. (2008) How do child and family social workers talk to parents about child welfare concerns?, *Child Abuse Review*, 17 (1): 23–35.

Foucault, M. (1972) *Archaeology of Knowledge*. Abingdon: Routledge.

Freidson, E. (1994) *Professionalism Reborn: Theory, Prophecy and Policy*. Cambridge: Polity Press.

Freidson, E. (2001) *Professionalism, the Third Logic*. Chicago, IL: The University of Chicago Press.

Garrett, P.M. (2016) Questioning tales of 'ordinary magic': 'resilience' and neo-Liberal reasoning, *British Journal of Social Work*, 46 (7): 1909–1925.

Gast, L. and Bailey, M. (2014) *Mastering Communication in Social Work: From Understanding to Doing*. London: Jessica Kingsley.

Gillingham, P. and Humphreys, C. (2010) Child protection practitioners and decision making tools: observations and reflections from the front line, *British Journal of Social Work*, 40 (8): 2598–2616.

Glaister, A. (2008) Introducing critical practice, in A.W. Fraser and S. Matthews (eds.) *The Critical Practitioner in Social Work and Health Care*. London: Sage.

Godden, J. (2012) *Integration and disintegration of health and social care services: A Charter for Social Workers in integrated health and social services in England*. Birmingham: BASW. Available at: http://cdn.basw.co.uk/upload/basw_20153-4.pdf (accessed 21 March 2017).

Gould, N. and Baldwin, M. (2004) *Social Work, Critical Reflection and the Learning Organisation*. Aldershot: Ashgate.

Gower, S. (2011) How old are you? Ethical dilemmas in working with age-disputed young asylum seekers, *Practice*, 23 (5): 325–339.

Grant, L. and Kinman, G. (2012) Enhancing wellbeing in social work students: building resilience in the next generation, *Social Work Education*, 31 (5): 605–621.

Grant, L. and Kinman, G. (2014) *Developing Resilience for Social Work Practice*. Basingstoke: Palgrave Macmillan.

Grant, L., Kinman, G. and Alexander, K. (2014) What's all this talk about emotion? Developing emotional intelligence in social work students, *Social Work Education*, 33 (7): 874–889.

Hafford-Letchfield, T. (2010) *Social Care Management, Strategy and Business Planning*. London: Jessica Kingsley.

Hallett, C. (1983) Social workers: their role and tasks, *British Journal of Social Work*, 13 (1): 395–404.

Harris, J. (1970) Local Authority Social Services Act 1970, *The Modern Law Review*, 33 (5): 530–534. Available at: http://www.jstor.org/stable/1093915 (accessed 14 May 2018).

Harrison, K. and Ruch, G. (2007) Social work and the use of the self: on becoming and being a social worker, in M. Lymbery and K. Postle (eds.) *Social Work: A Companion to Learning*. London: Sage.

Health and Care Professions Council (HCPC) (2017) *Continuing professional development and your registration*. London: HCPC. Available at: http://www.hcpc-uk.org/assets/documents/10001314CPD_and_your_registration.pdf (accessed 15 January 2018).

Health and Safety Executive (HSE) (2016) *Work related stress, anxiety and depression statistics in Great Britain 2016*. London: HSE. Available at: http://www.hse.gov.uk/statistics/causdis/stress/stress.pdf?pdf=stress (accessed 20 August 2017).

Healy, K. and Meagher, G. (2004) The reprofessionalization of social work: collaborative approaches for achieving professional recognition, *British Journal of Social Work*, 34 (2): 243–260.

Hebb, J. (2013) Social work values are essential in my work with high risk offenders, *Community Care*, 2 April. Available at: http://www.communitycare.co.uk/2013/04/02/social-work-values-are-essential-in-my-work-with-high-risk-offenders (accessed 19 August 2017).

Helen Sanderson Associates (n.d.) *Person-centred practices: Maps*. Stockport: HSA. Available at: http://helensandersonassociates.co.uk/person-centred-practice/maps/ (accessed 21 August 2017).

Hicks, L., Gibbs, I., Weatherly, H. et al. (2009) Management, leadership and resources in children's homes: what influences outcomes in residential child-care settings?, *British Journal of Social Work*, 39 (5): 828–845.

Higham, P. (2013) Understanding continuing professional development, in J. Parker and M. Doel (eds.) *Professional Social Work*. London: Sage.

Hingley-Jones, H. and Ruch, G. (2016) 'Stumbling through'? Relationship-based social work practice in austere times, *Journal of Social Work Practice*, 30 (3): 235–248.

HM Government (2015) *Working together to safeguard children*. Available at: https://www.gov.uk/government/publications/working-together-to-safeguard-children--2 (accessed 17 January 2018).

Hohman, M. (2012) *Motivational Interviewing in Social Work*. New York: Guilford Press.

Holland, S., Forrester, D., Williams, A. et al. (2014) Parenting and substance misuse: understanding accounts and realities in child protection contexts, *British Journal of Social Work*, 44 (6): 1491–1507.

Holroyd, J. (2015) *Self-leadership and Personal Resilience in Health and Social Care*. Exeter: Learning Matters.

Hopkinson, P.J., Killick, M., Batish, A. et al. (2015) 'Why didn't we do this before?' The development of Making Safeguarding Personal in the London borough of Sutton, *Journal of Adult Protection*, 17 (3): 181–194.

Howe, D. (2008) *The Emotionally Intelligent Social Worker*. Basingstoke: Palgrave Macmillan.

Hussein, S., Moriarty, J., Stevens, M. et al. (2014) Organisational factors, job satisfaction and intention to leave among newly qualified social workers in England, *Social Work Education*, 33 (3): 381–396.

Ingram, R. (2013) Locating emotional intelligence at the heart of social work practice, *British Journal of Social Work*, 43 (5): 987–1004.

International Federation of Social Workers (IFSW) (2014) *Global definition of social work*. Berne: IFSW. Available at: http://ifsw.org/get-involved/global-definition-of-social-work/ (accessed 28 August 2017).

Jones, C. (2001) Voices from the front line: state social workers and New Labour, *British Journal of Social Work*, 31 (4): 547–562.

Jones, K. and Watson, S. (2013) *Best Practice with Older People: Social Work Stories*. Basingstoke: Palgrave Macmillan.

Judd, R.G. and Sheffield, S. (2010) Hospital social work: contemporary roles and professional activities, *Social Work in Health Care*, 49 (9): 856–871.

Karban, K. and Smith, S. (2010) Developing critical reflection within an inter-professional learning programme, in H. Bradbury, N. Frost, S. Kilminster and M. Zukas (eds.) *Beyond Reflective Practice: New Approaches to Professional Lifelong Learning*. London: Routledge.

Keddell, E. (2014) Theorising the signs of safety approach to child protection social work: positioning, codes and power, *Children and Youth Services Review*, 47 (1): 70–77.

Kemshall, H. (2013) Risk assessment and risk management, in M. Davies (ed.) *The Blackwell Companion to Social Work*, 4th edn. Chichester: Wiley-Blackwell.

Kinman, G. and Grant, L. (2011) Exploring stress resilience in trainee social workers: the role of emotional and social competencies, *British Journal of Social Work*, 2 (1): 261–275.

Kinman, G., Wray, S. and Strange, C. (2011) Emotional labour, burnout and job satisfaction in UK teachers: the role of workplace social support, *Educational Psychology*, 31 (7): 843–856.

Kondrat, D.C. (2014) Person-centred approach, in B. Teater, *An Introduction to Applying Social Work Theories and Methods*, 2nd edn. Maidenhead: Open University Press.

Koprowska, J. (2014) *Communication and Interpersonal Skills in Social Work*, 4th edn. London: Sage.

Lambley, S. and Marrable, T. (2013) *Practice enquiry into supervision in a variety of adult care settings where there are health and social care practitioners working together.* London: SCIE. Available at: http://www.scie.org.uk/publications/guides/guide50/index.asp (accessed 21 August 2017).

Laming, H. (2009) *The Protection of Children in England: A Progress Report.* London: The Stationery Office.

Langfred, C.W. (2007) The downside of self-management: a longitudinal study of the effects of conflict on trust, autonomy, and task interdependence in self-managing teams, *Academy of Management Journal*, 50 (4): 885–900.

LaVigna, G.W. and Donnellan, A.M. (1986) *Alternatives to Punishment: Solving Behavior Problems with Nonaversive Strategies.* New York: Irvington Publishers.

Lawler, J. (2007) Leadership in social work: a case of caveat emptor?, *British Journal of Social Work*, 37 (1): 123–141.

Lawson, J., Lewis, S. and Williams, C. (2014a) *Making Safeguarding Personal: 2013/2014 Summary of Findings.* London: Local Government Association.

Lawson, J., Lewis, S. and Williams, C. (2014b) *Making Safeguarding Personal: Guide 2014.* London: Local Government Association.

Lefevre, M. (2008) Communicating and engaging with children and young people in care through play and the creative arts, in B. Luckock and M. Lefevre (eds.) *Direct Work: Social Work with Children and Young People in Care.* London: BAAF.

Local Government Association (LGA) (2014) *Making Safeguarding Personal 2013/14: Selection of tools used by participating councils.* London: LGA. Available at: https://www.local.gov.uk/sites/default/files/documents/Making%20Safeguarding%20Personal%202013-2014%20-%20Selection%20of%20tools%20used%20by%20participating%20councils.pdf (accessed 25 March 2018).

Local Government Association (LGA) (2018) *Making Safeguarding Personal.* London: LGA. Available at: https://www.local.gov.uk/topics/social-care-health-and-integration/adult-social-care/making-safeguarding-personal (accessed 5 January 2018).

Locke, E.A. and Latham, G.P. (2002) Building a practically useful theory of goal setting and task motivation: a 35-year odyssey, *American Psychologist*, 59 (9): 705–717.

Lorig, K.R. and Holman, H.R. (2003) Self-management education: history, definition, outcomes, and mechanisms, *Annals of Behavorial Medicine*, 26 (1): 1–7.

Makaton Charity (n.d.) *How Makaton works.* Farnborough: The Makaton Charity. Available at: https://www.makaton.org/aboutMakaton/howMakatonWorks (accessed 3 September 2017).

Manthorpe, J., Moriarty, J., Rapaport, J. et al. (2008) There are wonderful social workers but it's a lottery: older people's views about social workers, *British Journal of Social Work*, 38 (6): 1132–1150.

Matthews, S. (2015) Practice example: the approved mental health professional as an advocate, *Community Care*, 23 November. Available at: http://www.communitycare.co.uk/2015/11/23/practice-example-approved-mental-health-professional-advocate/ (accessed 20 August 2017).

McAllister, M. and McKinnon, T. (2009) The importance of teaching and learning resilience in the health disciplines: a critical review of the literature, *Nurse Education Today*, 29 (4): 371–379.

McCleskey, J.A. (2014) Situational, transformational, and transactional leadership and leadership development, *Journal of Business Studies Quarterly*, 5 (4): 117–130.

McFadden, P., Campbell, A. and Taylor, B. (2015) Resilience and burnout in child protection social work: individual and organisational themes from a systematic literature review, *British Journal of Social Work*, 45 (2): 1546–1563.

McLaughlin, H. (2009) What's in a name: 'client', 'patient', 'customer', 'consumer', 'expert by experience', 'service user' – what's next?, *British Journal of Social Work*, 39 (6): 1101–1117.

McLean, R. (2017) *Iriss on ... Risk*. Glasgow: Iriss. Available at: https://www.iriss.org.uk/resources/irisson/risk (accessed 22 August 2017).

McNicoll, A. (2013) This profession should be challenging prejudice, not telling social workers to hide their sexuality, *Community Care*. Available at: http://www.communitycare.co.uk/blogs/mental-health/2013/07/this-profession-should-be-challenging-prejudice-not-telling-social-workers-to-hide-their-sexuality/ (accessed 20 August 2017).

Miller, L. (2005) *Counselling Skills for Social Work*. London: Sage.

Miller, S.E. (2010) A conceptual framework for the professional socialization of social workers, *Journal of Human Behavior in the Social Environment*, 20 (7): 924–938.

Miller, W.R. and Rose, G.S. (2009) Toward a theory of motivational interviewing, *American Psychologist*, 64 (6): 527–537.

Mills, S. (2004). *Discourse*. London: Routledge.

Mitchell, W. and Glendinning, C. (2008) Risk and adult social care: identification, management and new policies. What does UK research evidence tell us?, *Health, Risk and Society*, 10 (3): 297–315.

Moran, P., Jacobs, C., Bunn, A. and Bifulco, A. (2007) Multi-agency working: implications for an early-intervention social work team, *Child and Family Social Work*, 12 (2): 143–151.

Morrison, T. (2007) Emotional intelligence, emotion and social work: context, characteristics, complications and contribution, *British Journal of Social Work*, 37 (2): 245–263.

Morrow, G., Burford, B., Rothwell, C. et al. (2014) *Professionalism in Healthcare Professionals*. London: Health and Care Professions Council.

Munby, J. (n.d.) *View from the president's chambers (3). The process of reform: Expert evidence*. Available at: https://www.judiciary.gov.uk/wp-content/uploads/JCO/Documents/FJC/Publications/VIEW+President+Expert(3).pdf (accessed 10 January 2018).

Munro, E. (1999) Common errors of reasoning in child protection work, *Child Abuse and Neglect*, 23 (8): 745–758.

Munro, E. (2011) *The Munro Review of Child Protection: Final Report, a child-centred system*. Available at: https://www.gov.uk/government/publications/munro-review-of-child-protection-final-report-a-child-centred-system (accessed 22 August 2017).

Nancarrow, S., Enderby, P., Ariss, S. et al. (2012) *Enhancing the effectiveness of interdisciplinary team working*, Final Report. NIHR Service Delivery and Organisation Programme. Available at: http://www.netscc.ac.uk/hsdr/files/project/SDO_A1_08-1819-214_V01.pdf. (accessed 26 July 2018)

National Association of Social Workers (NASW) (2012) *Career coaching: A valuable resource for social workers*. Washington, DC: NASW. Available at: http://careers.socialworkers.org/documents/careercoaching.pdf (accessed 11 August 2017).

Needham, K. (2015) The importance of small steps: making safeguarding personal in North Somerset, *Journal of Adult Protection*, 17 (3): 166–172.

Oliver, B. and Pitt, B. (2013) *Engaging Communities and Service Users: Context, Themes and Methods*. Basingstoke: Palgrave Macmillan.

Orme, J. and Shemmings, D. (2010) *Developing Research Based Social Work Practice*. Basingstoke: Palgrave.

Oxfordshire Safeguarding Children Board (2016) *Child J – Domestic Homicide Review and Serious Case Review (combined): Report into the death of Child J aged 17*. Available at: http://www.oscb.org.uk/wp-content/uploads/Child-J-OSCB-Overview-Report.pdf (accessed 30 August 2017).

Paley S. (2013) *Promoting Positive Behaviour when Supporting People with a Learning Disability and People with Autism*. Kidderminster: BILD.

Payne, M. (2005) *Modern Social Work Theory*. Basingstoke: Palgrave Macmillan.

Payne, M. (2006) *What is Professional Social Work?* Bristol: Policy Press.

Payne, M. (2013) Being a social work professional, in J. Parker and M. Doel (eds.) *Professional Social Work*. London: Learning Matters.

Peters, S.C. (2017) Defining social work leadership: a theoretical and conceptual review and analysis, *Journal of Social Work Practice* [doi: 10.1080/02650533.2017.1300877].

Pike, L. and Walsh, J. (2015) *Making Safeguarding Personal 2014/15: Evaluation report*. London: Local Government Association. Available at: https://www.local.gov.uk/topics/social-care-health-and-integration/adult-social-care/making-safeguarding-personal

Prochaska, J.O., DiClemente, C.O. and Norcross, J.C. (1992) In search of how people change: applications to addictive behaviours, *American Psychologist*, 47 (9): 1102–1114.

Prochaska, J.O., Velicer, W.F., Rossi, J.S. et al. (1994) Stages of change and decisional balance for 12 problem behaviors, *Health Psychology*, 13 (1): 39–46.

Ray, M., Pugh, R., Roberts, D. et al. (2008) *Mental health and social work*, SCIE Research Briefing 26. London: SCIE. Available at: http://www.scie.org.uk/publications/briefings/briefing26/ (accessed 22 August 2017).

Resolutions Consultancy (2017) *Signs of Safety*. Available at: https://www.signsofsafety.net/signs-of-safety/ (accessed 5 January 2018).

Rogers, C. (1961) *On Becoming a Person*. Boston, MA: Houghton Mifflin.

Rogers, M., Dawn, W., Edmonson, D. et al. (2017) *Developing Skills for Social Work Practice*. London: Sage.

Rogowski, S. (2011) Social work with children and families: challenges and possibilities in the neo-liberal world, *British Journal of Social Work*, 42 (5): 921–940.

Rollnick, S. and Allison, J. (2004) Motivational interviewing, in N. Heather and T. Stockwell (eds.) *The Essential Handbook of Treatment and Prevention of Alcohol Problems*. Chichester: Wiley.

Rollnick, S. and Miller W.R. (1995) What is motivational interviewing?, *Behavioural and Cognitive Psychotherapy*, 23 (4): 325–334.

Rollnick, S., Butler, C.C., Kinnersley, P. et al. (2010) Motivational interviewing, *British Medical Journal*, 340: c1900.

Romeo, L. (2014) Social workers need to get back to research, *The Guardian*, 9 April. Available at: https://www.theguardian.com/social-care-network/2014/apr/09/lyn-romeo-social-workers-research (accessed 20 August 2017).

Romeo, L. (2015) Social work and safeguarding adults, *Journal of Adult Protection*, 17 (3): 205–207.

Rose, N. and Miller, P.(1992) Political power beyond the state: problematics of government, *British Journal of Sociology*, 43 (2): 173–205.

Ruch, G. (2007) Reflective practice in child care social work: the role of containment, *British Journal of Social Work*, 37 (4): 659–680.

Ruch, G., Turney, D. and Ward, A. (2010) *Relationship-based Social Work: Getting to the Heart of Practice*. London: Jessica Kingsley.

Ryan, P. and Swain, K.J. (2009) The Individual and Family Self-management Theory: background and perspectives on context, process, and outcomes, *Nursing Outlook*, 54 (7): 217–225.

Salovey, P. and Mayer, J.D. (1990) Emotional intelligence, *Imagination, Cognition, and Personality*, 9 (3): 185–211. Available at: http://dmcodyssey.org/wp-content/uploads/2013/09/EMOTIONAL-INTELLIGENCE-3.pdf (accessed 7 July 2017).

Saltiel, D. (2013) Understanding complexity in families' lives: the usefulness of 'family practices' as an aid to decision-making, *Child and Family Social Work*, 18 (1): 15–24.

Scholar, H., McLaughlin, H., McCaughan, S. et al. (2014) Learning to be a social worker in a non-traditional placement: critical reflections on social work, professional identity and social work education in England, *Social Work Education*, 33 (8): 998–1016.

Schunk, D.H. (1990) Goal setting and self-efficacy during self-regulated learning, *Educational Psychologist*, 25 (1): 71–86.

Shaw, I. (2009) Ways of knowing in social work, in M. Gray and S. Webb (eds.) *Social Work Theory and Method*. London: Sage.

Shaw, I., Bell, M., Sinclair, I. et al. (2009) An exemplary scheme? An evaluation of the Integrated Children's System, *British Journal of Social Work*, 39 (4): 613–626.

Singh, S.K. (2006) Social work professionals' emotional intelligence, locus of control and role efficacy: an exploratory study, *Journal of Human Resource Management*, 4 (2): 39–45.

Smith, M. (2004) *Surviving Fears in Health and Social Care: The Terrors of Night and the Arrows of Day*. London: Jessica Kingsley.

Smith, R. (2008) *Social Work and Power*. Basingstoke: Palgrave Macmillan.

Smith, R. (2009) *Doing Social Work Research*. Maidenhead: Open University Press.

Social Care Institute for Excellence (SCIE) (2013) *Effective supervision in a variety of settings*. London: SCIE. Available at: http://www.scie.org.uk/publications/guides/guide50/index.asp (accessed 21 August 2017).

Social Work Reform Board (SWRB) (2010) *Building a safe and confident future: One year on*. Available at: https://www.gov.uk/government/uploads/system/uploads/attachment_data/file/180787/DFE-00602-2010-1.pdf (accessed 10 January 2018).

Social Work Task Force (SWTF) (2009) *Building a safe, confident future: the final report of the Social Work Taskforce*. Available at: http://webarchive.nationalarchives.gov.uk/20130403221302/https://www.education.gov.uk/publications/eOrderingDownload/01114-2009DOM-EN.pdf (accessed 21 August 2017).

Stanley, T. (2016) A practice framework to support the Care Act 2014, *Journal of Adult Protection*, 18 (1): 53–64.

Stokes, J. and Schmidt, G. (2012) Child protection decision making: a factorial analysis using case vignettes, *Social Work*, 57 (1): 83–90.

Stone, A.G., Russell, R.F. and Patterson, K. (2004) Transformational versus servant leadership: a difference in leader focus, *Leadership and Organisational Development Journal*, 25 (4): 349–361.

Stone, C. (2016) The role of practice educators in initial and post qualifying social worker education, *Social Work Education*, 35 (6): 706–718.

Tafvelin, S., Hyvönen, U. and Westerberg, K. (2014) Transformational leadership in the social work context: the importance of leader continuity and co-worker support, *British Journal of Social Work*, 44 (4): 886–904.

Taylor, B. (2013) *Professional Decision Making and Risk in Social Work*, 2nd edn. London: Sage.

Taylor, I. and Bogo, M. (2014) Perfect opportunity – perfect storm? Raising the standards of social work education in England, *British Journal of Social Work*, 44 (6): 1402–1418.

Taylor, M.F. (2007) Professional dissonance, *Smith College Studies in Social Work*, 77 (1): 89–99 [doi: 10.1300/J497v77n01_0].

Tew, J. (2006) Understanding power and powerlessness: towards a framework for emancipatory practice in social work, *Journal of Social Work*, 6 (1): 33–51.

The College of Social Work (2015) *Review of the Professional Capabilities Framework (PCF)*, Final Report. Available at: https://www.basw.co.uk/pcf/pcfreview2015.pdf (accessed 9 May 2018).

Thompson, N. (2011) *Effective Communication: A Guide for the People Professions*, 2nd edn. Basingstoke: Palgrave Macmillan.

Thompson, N. (2016) *The Professional Social Worker*, 2nd edn. Basingstoke: Palgrave Macmillan.

Thompson, N. (2017) *Social Problems and Social Justice*. Basingstoke: Palgrave Macmillan.

Thompson, R. (2011) Using life story work to enhance care, *Nursing Older People*, 23 (8): 16–21.

TNS BMRB (2015) *Attitudes to Mental Illness 2014 Research Report*. Available at: https://www.time-to-change.org.uk/sites/default/files/Attitudes_to_mental_illness_2014_report_final_0.pdf (accessed 22 August 2017).

Tompsett, H., Henderson, K., Mathew B.J. et al. (2017) Self-efficacy and outcomes: validating a measure comparing social work students' perceived and assessed ability in core pre-placement skills, *British Journal of Social Work*, 47 (8): 2384–2405.

Trevithick, P. (2003) Effective relationship-based practice: a theoretical exploration, *Journal of Social Work Practice*, 17 (2): 173–186.

Turnell, A. and Edwards, S. (1999) *Signs of Safety: A Solution and Safety Oriented Approach to Child Protection Casework*. New York: W.W. Norton.

Turnell, A. and Murphy, T. (2017) *Signs of Safety® Comprehensive Briefing Paper*, 4th edn. East Perth, WA: Resolutions Consultancy.

Turney, D. (2014) *Analysis and critical thinking in assessment: Literature review*. Available at: https://www.rip.org.uk/resources/publications/research-reviews-and-summaries/analysis-and-critical-thinking-in-assessment-literature-review-2014/ (accessed 20 August 2017).

Turney, D., Platt, D., Selwyn, J. et al. (2011) *Social work assessment of children in need: What do we know? Messages from research*. Available at: https://www.gov.uk/government/publications/social-work-assessment-of-children-in-need-what-do-we-know-messages-from-research (accessed 22 August 2017).

Uhl-Bien, M. and Graen, G.B. (1998) Individual self-management: analysis of professionals' self-managing activities in functional and cross-functional work teams, *Academy of Management Journal*, 41 (3): 340–350.

University of Massachusetts Amherst (n.d.) *A definition of motivational interviewing*. Available at: https://www.umass.edu/studentlife/sites/default/files/documents/pdf/Motivational_Interviewing_Definition_Principles_Approach.pdf (accessed 17 September 2017).

Wahab, S. (2005) Motivational interviewing and social work practice, *Journal of Social Work*, 5 (1): 45–60.

Waldman, D.A., Javidan, M. and Varella, P. (2004) Charismatic leadership at the strategic level: a new application of upper echelons theory, *Leadership Quarterly*, 15 (3): 355–380.

Walpole, B., Dettmer, E., Morrongiello, B.A. et al. (2013) Motivational interviewing to enhance self-efficacy and promote weight loss in overweight and obese adolescents: a randomized controlled trial, *Journal of Pediatric Psychology*, 38 (9): 944–953.

Warner, J. (2006) Community care and the location and governance of risk in mental health, *Forum: Qualitative Social Research*, 7 (1). Available at: http://www.qualitative-research.net/index.php/fqs/article/view/59/121 (accessed 22 August 2017).

Webb, S.A. (2006) *Social Work in a Risk Society: Social and Political Perspectives*. Basingstoke: Palgrave Macmillan.

Weinberg, M. (2005) A case for an expanded framework of ethics in practice, *Ethics and Behavior*, 15 (4): 327–338.

Weld, N. (2008) The three houses tool: building safety and positive change, in M. Calder (ed.) *Contemporary Risk Assessment in Safeguarding Children*. Lyme Regis: Russell House Publishing.

White, S. and Featherstone, B. (2005) Communicating misunderstandings: multi-agency work as social practice, *Child and Family Social Work*, 10 (3): 207–216.

Whittaker, K.A., Cox, P., Thomas, N. et al. (2014) A qualitative study of parents' experiences using family support services: applying the concept of surface and depth, *Health and Social Care in the Community*, 22 (5): 479–487.

Whittington, C. (2006) *Social care governance: A report commissioned by SCIE for the joint project with the Northern Ireland Clinical and Social Care Governance Support Team*. Available at: http://www.whittingtonconsultants.co.uk/media/Social+Care+Governance_SCIE_Final_cw110406_sharedcpy160309.pdf (accessed 28 August 2017).

Wiles, F. (2017) What is professional identity and how do social workers acquire it?, in S.A. Webb (ed.) *Professional Identity and Social Work*. London: Routledge.

Wilkins, D. (2015) Balancing risk and protective factors: how do social workers and social work managers analyse referrals that may indicate children are at risk of significant harm?, *British Journal of Social Work*, 45 (1): 395–411.

Wilkins, D. and Boahen, G. (2013) *Critical Analysis Skills for Social Workers*. Maidenhead: Open University Press.

Winkler, I. (2009) *Contemporary Leadership Theories: Contributions to Management Science*. Dordrecht: Springer.

Zeira, A. and Rosen, A. (2000) Unraveling 'tacit knowledge': what social workers do and why they do it, *Social Service Review*, 74 (1): 103–123.

Index